Build Websites with AI

A Beginner's Guide to Front-End Coding using AI

By Laurence Lars Svekis

Dedicated to

Alexis and Sebastian

Thank you for your support

For more content and to learn more, visit
https://basescripts.com

Introduction – Building Websites with AI for Everyone

In this chapter, we set the stage by explaining why building websites is an essential skill, how AI can simplify the learning process, and why you don't need a technical background to succeed. We'll also discuss the exciting outcomes you can expect from this journey, including the websites you'll be able to create by the end of this guide.

Learning Objectives

By the end of this chapter, you will be able to:

- **Understand the Importance of Building Websites:**

    - Recognize the impact and benefits of having web development skills.

    - Learn how creating websites can enhance personal and professional opportunities.

- **Comprehend How AI Simplifies Web Development:**

    - Identify the advantages of using AI tools to generate code and solve design challenges.

    - Understand how AI acts as a supportive learning partner, turning complex coding concepts into approachable tasks.

- **Realize You Don't Need a Tech Background:**

- Overcome common fears of starting with no technical expertise.

- Appreciate that anyone can learn web development step by step through guided examples and practice.

- **Envision What You'll Create:**

  - Get an overview of the types of websites and projects you'll be able to build by the end of this guide.

  - Build excitement and confidence by seeing real-world examples and project ideas.

Section 1: Why Build Websites?

Explanation

Websites are the heart of the digital world. They serve as online resumes, business hubs, communication platforms, and creative outlets. Whether you're looking to promote your brand, share your creative work, or launch an online business, a website is essential.

Key Benefits:

- **Global Reach:** Your website can be accessed by anyone, anywhere in the world.

- **Professional Presence:** It establishes credibility and can serve as an online portfolio or resume.

- **Creative Expression:** It is a canvas for presenting your ideas, projects, and interests.

- **Opportunities:** Opens doors to freelance work, job opportunities, and collaborations.

Real-World Examples

- A freelancer uses their personal website as a portfolio to showcase projects, attracting potential clients.

- A small business creates a site to display products and information, reaching customers without investing in costly advertising.

- A blogger reaches a global audience with their creative writing and multimedia content.

Exercise & Action Items

Exercise:
Think about your own reasons for wanting to build a website. Write down three personal or professional goals you could achieve with your website.

Action Item:

- Create a brainstorming document or a simple mind map outlining why building a website is important to you. List potential benefits and personal goals.

Checklist:

- Identify personal or professional goals for building a website.

- Note at least three benefits of owning a website.

- Visualize how a website could help achieve your objectives.

Section 2: How AI Makes Learning Web Development Easy

Explanation

Artificial Intelligence is revolutionizing the way we learn and build websites. AI-powered tools can generate HTML, CSS, and JavaScript code based on simple prompts, assist with debugging, and even offer design inspirations. This technology significantly reduces the time and effort needed to code from scratch.

Advantages of Using AI:

- **Instant Code Generation:** Get a quick starting point by asking AI to produce code snippets.

- **Learning by Example:** See practical implementations of code and learn best practices by reviewing AI outputs.

- **Error Reduction:** AI helps catch common mistakes and improve the quality of your code.

- **Customization:** Use AI-generated code as a foundation that you can modify and personalize as you learn.

Real-World Examples

- Using online tools like ChatGPT or Codex to generate a responsive navigation bar.

- AI suggesting color schemes and layout ideas that are modern and visually appealing.

- Debugging code with the help of AI by describing an issue and receiving targeted fixes.

Exercise & Action Items

Exercise:
Write a simple prompt for AI to generate HTML code for a basic webpage. For instance:

> "Generate HTML code for a webpage with a header, a paragraph introducing my portfolio, and a footer with contact information."

Action Item:

- Use an online AI tool to generate the code based on your prompt.

- Compare the generated code with simple examples provided in this guide.

- Experiment by modifying some of the code to better suit your personal style.

Checklist:

- Experiment with at least one AI code-generation prompt.

- Review and analyze the provided code.

- Modify the generated code to match your preferences.

- Document what you learned from this process.

Section 3: You Don't Need a Tech Background (Promise!)

Explanation

One of the biggest obstacles for beginners is the misconception that you must have a technical background to build websites. The truth is, web development is accessible to everyone. This guide is designed for non-coders with no prior experience. With AI's supportive capabilities, the learning process is transformed into a series of manageable, enjoyable steps.

Key Points:

- **Step-by-Step Approach:** Learn through simple examples, exercises, and customization.

- **Supportive AI Tools:** Rely on AI to provide code examples, suggestions, and debugging help.

- **Community and Resources:** Countless tutorials, forums, and guides are available to help you.

- **Hands-On Practice:** You'll gain confidence with interactive projects and real-world applications.

Real-World Examples

- A complete beginner starts by generating a basic webpage using AI without any prior coding experience and later builds a personal portfolio.

- Individuals from non-tech backgrounds create websites for small businesses, hobbies, or personal blogs by following guided tutorials and using AI assistance.

Exercise & Action Items

Exercise:
List three common misconceptions you had about web development before starting this guide and write a brief explanation of how your perspective has changed.

Action Item:

- Create a "My Web Journey" journal entry where you describe your background and your initial thoughts about coding. Revisit this entry as you progress and note your improvements and new skills.

Checklist:

- Identify and debunk three common myths about web development.

- Write a personal journal entry outlining your previous assumptions versus your new understanding.

- Reflect on how AI is making your learning process more approachable.

Section 4: What You'll Be Able to Create by the End

Explanation

As you work through this guide, you will gain the skills needed to build fully functional, aesthetically pleasing websites using HTML, CSS, and JavaScript. By the end of your journey, you'll be able to create a variety of websites that range from personal portfolios to interactive web applications.

Projects You Will Be Able to Build:

- **Personal Portfolio Page:** Showcase your projects, skills, and background.

- **Simple Landing Pages:** Create promotional pages for products, events, or businesses.

- **Interactive Websites:** Develop projects like quiz games and photo galleries that engage users.

- **Multi-Page Sites:** Learn to organize content across several linked pages, complete with responsive design.

Real-World Examples

- **Portfolio Website:** A visually engaging site that contains sections like About, Projects, and Contact, demonstrating not only your work but also your growing technical skills.

- **Landing Page:** A focused page for a new product launch that features a striking hero image, clear call-to-action buttons, and responsive design for mobile devices.

- **Interactive Quiz Game:** A fun and engaging web application that uses JavaScript to validate answers and provide instant feedback.

- **Photo Gallery:** A sleek gallery with a lightbox effect that allows users to click on thumbnails and view larger images, showcasing your creative design skills.

Exercise & Action Items

Exercise:
Sketch a rough layout on paper for a website you would like to create by the end of this course.

- Include sections such as a header, body, and footer.

- Identify interactive elements like buttons or forms.

Action Item:

- Write a list of features and elements you want your final project to include.

- Use this list as a roadmap for your learning journey and as a goal to work toward.

Checklist:

- Determine the type of website you want to create.

- List the core components (e.g., header, navigation, content sections, footer).

- Identify interactive features you plan to include (e.g., forms, animations, quizzes).

- Set clear, achievable goals for your final project.

Summary

In this introductory chapter, you've learned why building websites is valuable, how AI can simplify the learning process, and why you don't need any tech background to get started. We've also set exciting expectations for the types of websites you'll be able to create by the end of this guide. Embrace the journey; every line of code and each project will build your confidence and ability to innovate in the digital world.

Final Action Items

1. **Reflect on Your Goals:**

   - Write down your personal and professional goals for building a website.

   - Consider how having an online presence can enhance opportunities for you.

2. **Experiment with AI Prompts:**

   - Try out an AI prompt to generate HTML or CSS code.

   - Modify the output to personalize it, then review what you've learned about each code section.

3. **Document Your Journey:**

- Maintain a journal or digital document where you record your progress, challenges, and successes.

- Update your journal regularly with your reflections on how your skills are growing.

4. **Plan Your Final Project:**

- Create a detailed list of features and designs for the website you want to build by the end.

- Use sketches or wireframes to visualize your project's layout.

Final Checklist:

- Understand why web development is a key skill.

- Recognize the benefits of using AI to simplify learning.

- Accept that no technical background is required to start coding.

- Identify the types of websites you'll be able to build.

- Set clear learning goals and document your progress.

- Experiment with initial AI prompts and modify the code for personalization.

By following these instructions and exercises, you're well on your way to becoming a proficient website builder using AI tools. Remember, every expert started as a beginner, and your journey has just begun. Enjoy the process, be patient with your progress, and keep building — one line of code at a time!

Chapter 1: What is Front-End Development?

In this chapter, we'll explore the essential building blocks for creating websites: HTML, CSS, and JavaScript. Whether you're completely new to coding or just curious about how websites come to life, this chapter is designed to be your friendly guide. We'll explain core concepts with real-world examples, guide you through practical exercises, and offer checklists to help you track your progress along the way.

Learning Objectives

By the end of this chapter, you will be able to:

- **Understand Front-End Development:** Define what front-end development is and why it's essential for building websites.

- **Describe Key Technologies:**

    ○ Explain the role of **HTML** in creating the structure of a webpage.

    ○ Explain the role of **CSS** in styling a webpage.

    ○ Explain the role of **JavaScript** in making a webpage interactive.

- **Explain How Websites Work:** Learn the simplified process of how a browser displays a website.

- **Explore Real-World Examples:** Recognize practical examples of websites and user interfaces that are built using these technologies.

- **Engage in Hands-On Practice:**

    - Complete exercises to reinforce your learning.

    - Follow action items and checklists to track and apply your new skills.

Section 1: What is Front-End Development?

Front-end development focuses on the parts of a website that users see and interact with. It involves coding and designing the layout, style, and interactive features of a website. This is where HTML, CSS, and JavaScript come into play.

1.1 Understanding HTML

HTML (HyperText Markup Language) is the backbone of any website. It provides the structure of your webpage by using elements known as tags. Think of HTML as the blueprint or skeleton of your website.

- **Basic Elements:**

    - `<html>`: Encloses the entire document.

- <head>: Contains metadata, the title, and links to stylesheets.

- <body>: Contains all the content visible on the webpage, such as text, images, links, and more.

Real-World Example:
Imagine a newspaper article. The headline, paragraphs, images, and even the labels on graphics are all structured using HTML. Each element (like <h1> for headlines or <p> for paragraphs) tells the browser how to display the content.

Checklist for HTML Basics:

- Understand the role of the <html>, <head>, and <body> tags.

- Practice using headings (<h1> to <h6>), paragraphs (<p>), and lists (<ul>, <ol>, <li>).

- Create a simple HTML page that includes a title, a header, a paragraph, and a list of three items.

1.2 Understanding CSS

CSS (Cascading Style Sheets) is used to style and layout your web pages. While HTML provides structure, CSS provides the design – colors, fonts, spacing, and overall look of the page.

Basic Syntax:
CSS rules are written in a "selector { property: value; }" format. For example:

```
body {
```

```
    background-color: #f0f0f0;
    font-family: Arial, sans-serif;
}
```

- This snippet tells the browser to set the background color of the page to a light grey and change the font of all text.

Real-World Example:
Think of CSS as the interior design of a house. While the structure (walls, windows) is provided by HTML, the décor (paint, furniture, layout) is handled by CSS.

Checklist for CSS Basics:

- Learn how to select HTML elements using selectors.

- Practice applying styles such as colors, fonts, margins, and paddings.

- Create a CSS file and connect it to your HTML file to see your styles in action.

1.3 Understanding JavaScript

JavaScript is the programming language that adds interactivity to your website. With JavaScript, you can create dynamic effects like animations, form validations, interactive maps, and much more.

- **Basic Concepts:**

  - Variables: Storing data.

  - Functions: Reusable blocks of code.

○   Events: Actions such as clicks or key presses that trigger functions.

Real-World Example:
Imagine clicking a button on a web store to add an item to your shopping cart. JavaScript powers such actions by responding to your click and updating the cart dynamically without reloading the page.

Checklist for JavaScript Basics:

- Understand how to declare variables (e.g., `let` and `const`).

- Write simple functions that perform specific tasks.

- Create an interactive element like a button that, when clicked, displays a message.

Section 2: How Websites Work (Simple Version)

Before diving deep into coding, it's important to understand how websites work at a fundamental level. Here's a step-by-step explanation of the process:

1. **User Request:**
   When you type a website address (URL) into your browser, you are sending a request to a server where the website is stored.

2. **Server Response:**
   The server responds by sending the website's files (HTML, CSS, JavaScript, images, etc.) back to your browser.

3. **Browser Rendering:**
   Your browser reads the HTML to understand the structure, applies the CSS for styling, and executes JavaScript to add interactivity. This process creates the visual webpage you interact with.

4. **Interaction:**
   As you click links, scroll, or input data, your browser might make additional requests to update or change parts of the webpage in real time.

Simplified Diagram (Text Version):

```
User Request → Server → Send Files → Browser
(HTML + CSS + JS) → Render Website → User
Interaction
```

Exercise:
 Create a simple flowchart on paper or using a drawing tool that illustrates these steps. Label each step clearly and consider what happens at each stage (e.g., "Sending request", "Receiving HTML file", "Rendering content").

Section 3: Real Examples of What You Can Build

Now that you know what HTML, CSS, and JavaScript are, let's look at some real-world examples of websites and interactive elements that you might build:

3.1 Simple Personal Website

- **Description:**
  Create a personal website to showcase your portfolio, resume, or blog.

- **Technologies Involved:**

  - **HTML:** Structure with headers, images, and text.

  - **CSS:** Custom styles to reflect your personality (colors, fonts, layout).

  - **JavaScript:** Interactive contact form and light/dark mode toggle.

- **Exercise:**
  Build a one-page website with an "About Me" section, a portfolio of projects, and a contact form. Use external CSS to style the page, and add a simple JavaScript function to display an alert when someone submits the form.

3.2 Interactive To-Do List Application

- **Description:**
  A dynamic web application where users can add, remove, and mark tasks as complete.

- **Technologies Involved:**

  - **HTML:** Create the structure for the list and input fields.

  - **CSS:** Style the list items, buttons, and overall layout.

  - **JavaScript:** Add functions to handle adding tasks, removing tasks, and toggling task completion.

- **Exercise:**
  Develop a simple to-do list app. Start with a static HTML layout, style it with CSS, and then write JavaScript to allow users to interact with the list in real time. Challenge yourself by adding a feature to save the list in the browser (using local storage).

3.3 Dynamic Landing Page for a Product

- **Description:**
  Create a landing page for a product that includes multimedia elements, interactive buttons, and smooth scrolling effects.

- **Technologies Involved:**

  - **HTML:** Layout sections such as hero, features, testimonials, and contact.

  - **CSS:** Design appealing and responsive sections.

  - **JavaScript:** Implement interactive elements like smooth scrolling navigation and dynamic modal pop-ups.

- **Exercise:**
  Design and code a landing page for your favorite product. Organize the content into sections and use JavaScript to create a navigation menu that smoothly scrolls to each section when clicked.

Action Items to Practice What You've Learned:

- **Action Item 1:**
  Build a Basic HTML Page:
  Create a new HTML file and build a simple webpage using essential HTML elements. Practice using headings, paragraphs, images, and links.

- **Action Item 2:**
  Style Your Page with CSS:
  Write a CSS file that targets your HTML elements. Experiment with different fonts, colors, and layouts until you create a visually appealing design.

- **Action Item 3:**
  Add JavaScript Interactivity:
  Write a small script that responds to a user action (like clicking a button) on your webpage. For example, display a welcome message or change the color of an element.

- **Action Item 4:**
  Combine the Skills:
  Merge your HTML, CSS, and JavaScript files into one project. Practice integrating these technologies by building a simple personal or portfolio website.

Checklist for Final Project:

- HTML page with a clear structure (header, body, footer)

- External CSS file linked properly

- JavaScript file for interactivity (at least one interactive element)

- At least one exercise completed from the examples above

Summary

In this chapter, you learned that front-end development involves creating the structure, style, and interactivity of a website through HTML, CSS, and JavaScript. We explored how these technologies work together and saw tangible examples of projects like personal websites, to-do lists, and landing pages. With the exercises, checklists, and action items provided, you are now equipped to start your own journey in front-end development using AI prompts and coding techniques.

Chapter 2: Setting Up Your Playground

In this chapter, we'll walk you through the easiest ways to write and test your code without installing any complex software. Whether you choose to use online editors like CodePen, Replit, or JSFiddle—or decide to dip your toes with Visual Studio Code—this chapter will guide you step-by-step. By the end, you'll also know how to run your very first web page and see your code come alive in the browser.

Learning Objectives

After completing this chapter, you will be able to:

- **Understand the Benefits of Online Code Editors:**

- Learn why online environments can make coding accessible and fun without the need for installations.

- **Explore Popular Online Code Editors:**

  - Gain an overview of CodePen, Replit, and JSFiddle with beginner-friendly guidance.

- **Set Up Visual Studio Code (Optional):**

  - Discover the basics of using Visual Studio Code as your coding environment.

- **Run Your First Web Page:**

  - Learn how to write HTML, CSS, and JavaScript code and view it immediately in your web browser.

- **Practice and Experiment:**

  - Engage with sample exercises and action items that reinforce key concepts and allow hands-on practice.

- **Track Your Progress:**

  - Use checklists to verify that you have completed each important step and concept.

Section 1: Easiest Ways to Write Code (No Installation Needed!)

For many beginners, the idea of installing software for coding can seem overwhelming. Fortunately, modern web development tools allow you to write and see your code in action directly from your browser.

1.1 The Benefits of Online Editors

- **Instant Setup:**
  No installation is required; just open a web browser and navigate to the website.

- **Live Preview:**
  See changes as you type and get instant feedback on your code.

- **Collaboration:**
  Many online editors allow you to share your project with friends or mentors, making it easy to get help or show off your work.

- **Accessibility:**
  They work on most devices and are ideal for beginners who want to experiment without commitment.

1.2 Popular Online Code Editors

Let's explore three popular online code editors:

CodePen

- **What It Is:**
  CodePen is a web-based editor where you can build, test, and showcase HTML, CSS, and JavaScript code in a user-friendly environment.

- **Real-World Example:**
  Imagine you want to create a visual effect like a hover animation. CodePen lets you quickly experiment with CSS animations and see the results right away.

- **Quick Exercise:**

    1. Visit CodePen.

    2. Click on **"Create"** to start a new pen.

    3. Write a simple HTML snippet, add some CSS to style it, and include a small piece of JavaScript to interact with an element.

    4. Observe the live preview on the right side of the screen.

Replit

- **What It Is:**
  Replit is an online coding environment that supports not only front-end languages (HTML, CSS, JavaScript) but also many backend languages. It's a great tool for those who want to build full-stack applications later on.

- **Real-World Example:**
  You could use Replit to create a simple interactive web game, combining your coding skills in a fun, integrated environment.

- **Quick Exercise:**

    1. Go to Replit.

2. Choose the "HTML, CSS, JavaScript" template.

3. Write some code that displays a welcome message on the webpage.

4. Use the provided live preview feature to see your site in action.

JSFiddle

- **What It Is:**
  JSFiddle is another lightweight online tool dedicated to quickly testing snippets of HTML, CSS, and JavaScript code.

- **Real-World Example:**
  If you're working on a small code snippet for a complex project, like testing a new JavaScript function or styling a button, JSFiddle is perfect for rapid prototyping.

- **Quick Exercise:**

  1. Open JSFiddle.

  2. Insert a simple HTML element (e.g., a button).

  3. Add CSS to style the button.

  4. Write JavaScript to display an alert when the button is clicked.

  5. Click **"Run"** and check out the immediate preview.

Checklist for Online Editor Setup:

- Visit CodePen, Replit, or JSFiddle.

- Create a new project or "pen."

- Write a small snippet of code in HTML, CSS, and/or JavaScript.

- Use the live preview to confirm your code works as expected.

Section 2: Visual Studio Code (Optional)

While online editors are fantastic for beginners and quick testing, many developers eventually choose a local development environment. Visual Studio Code (VS Code) is a free, robust, and highly customizable code editor that is popular in the industry.

2.1 Benefits of Using Visual Studio Code

- **Customizability:**
  With thousands of extensions, you can tailor VS Code to fit your workflow.

- **Powerful Tools:**
  Features like IntelliSense (code auto-completion) and debugging tools can save time and make coding easier.

- **Offline Development:**
  You can work on your projects without needing an internet connection.

2.2 Getting Started with Visual Studio Code

- **Installation:**
  Download VS Code from <u>Visual Studio Code</u>.
  (Installation instructions are available on the website, but for this chapter, exploring online editors is recommended if you prefer not to install any software.)

- **Exploring the Interface:**
  Familiarize yourself with the sidebar, editor area, and terminal — all essential parts of the development process.

- **Creating Your First File:**
  Open VS Code and create a new file named `index.html`. Start typing your HTML code and see the benefits of local development.

Exercise:

1. If you choose to install VS Code, follow the installation instructions on their website.

2. Create a new project folder on your computer.

3. Inside the folder, create three files: `index.html`, `styles.css`, and `script.js`.

4. Write a basic HTML file that links to your CSS and JavaScript files.

5. Open your HTML file in a browser to see your work.

Checklist for Visual Studio Code Setup (Optional):

- Download and install Visual Studio Code (if desired).

- Create a new project folder with `index.html`, `styles.css`, and `script.js`.

- Write a basic web page and link the CSS and JS files.

- Open the web page in your browser to test your setup.

Section 3: Running Your First Web Page

Now that you're familiar with different coding environments, it's time to run your first web page! This exercise will help you understand the process of turning code into something you can see and interact with in your browser.

3.1 Creating a Simple Web Page

Let's build a very simple web page using HTML, CSS, and JavaScript. Below is a step-by-step guide.

Step-by-Step Guide:
Write Your HTML:
Create an HTML file named `index.html`. Add the following code:

```
<!DOCTYPE html>
<html>
<head>
    <title>My First Web Page</title>
    <link rel="stylesheet"
href="styles.css">
</head>
<body>
    <h1>Welcome to My Web Page!</h1>
```

```
    <p>This is a simple web page built with
HTML, CSS, and JavaScript.</p>
    <button id="greetBtn">Click Me!</button>
    <script src="script.js"></script>
</body>
</html>
```

Style with CSS:

In your `styles.css` file, add some basic styling:

```
body {
    font-family: Arial, sans-serif;
    background-color: #f9f9f9;
    text-align: center;
    padding: 50px;
}
h1 {
    color: #333;
}
button {
    padding: 10px 20px;
    font-size: 16px;
    cursor: pointer;
}
```

Add JavaScript Interactivity:

In your `script.js` file, add a simple script to display a message when the button is clicked:

```
// Select the button element
const greetBtn =
document.getElementById('greetBtn');
// Add an event listener to the button
greetBtn.addEventListener('click',
function() {
    alert('Hello, welcome to your first web
page!');
});
```

1. **Test Your Web Page:**
   Open your `index.html` file in a web browser. You should see your styled page, and when you click the button, an alert should appear.

3.2 Real-World Example in Action

Imagine you're launching a simple landing page for an event. Your HTML lays out the event details, your CSS styles the page with a professional look, and your JavaScript adds a registration pop-up. The workflow is very similar to the simple web page you just created, but with additional content and features that make it dynamic and engaging.

Action Items to Practice What You've Learned:

- **Action Item 1: Build a Basic Web Page**
  Create your own `index.html`, `styles.css`, and `script.js` files and write a simple web page using the code examples above.

- **Action Item 2: Experiment with Styles**
  Change the background color, update the font, and adjust the padding in your CSS to see how it affects the layout.

- **Action Item 3: Enhance Interactivity**
  Modify the JavaScript code to display a custom message or change an element's color when the button is clicked.

Checklist for Running Your First Web Page:

- Create `index.html` with basic HTML structure.

- Add a linked `styles.css` file and write simple CSS rules.

- Write `script.js` to include basic interactivity.

- Open `index.html` in your browser to view your work.

- Test the interactive button to ensure it works correctly.

Summary

In this chapter, you learned how to set up your coding playground using online editors like CodePen, Replit, and JSFiddle, as well as an optional introduction to Visual Studio Code. You discovered the benefits of these tools, learned to run your first web page, and practiced by creating a simple project. With checklists, exercises, and action items, you now have a clear path to experiment and build confidence in your front-end coding skills.

Chapter 3: Meeting Your AI Website Builder Assistant

In this chapter, we'll explore the exciting world of AI-powered website building. We'll show you how to use AI to write website code, provide tips on asking the right questions, and clarify what AI can — and can't — do for you. This chapter is packed with practical examples, exercises, and actionable checklists to help you build confidence and mastery over using AI as your coding assistant.

Learning Objectives

By the end of this chapter, you will be able to:

- **Understand How AI Can Help with Website Code:**

    - Explain the ways in which AI tools can generate HTML, CSS, and JavaScript code.

    - Recognize real-world scenarios where AI accelerates your coding process.

- **Ask AI the Right Questions:**

    - Learn effective strategies for communicating with AI.

    - Discover tips for refining your AI prompts to get the best results.

- **Know the Capabilities and Limitations of AI:**

    - Identify tasks that AI is ideally suited for in web development.

- Understand what AI may struggle with and when human expertise is required.

- **Apply What You Learn Through Exercises:**

  - Engage in sample exercises that let you practice crafting prompts.

  - Follow action items and checklists to ensure you've grasped each concept.

Section 1: How AI Can Help You Write Website Code

AI tools have revolutionized the way we approach coding, especially for beginners. These tools provide assistance by generating code snippets, correcting errors, and offering suggestions based on your inputs. Here's what AI can do for you:

1.1 AI-Powered Code Generation

- **Instant Code Snippets:**
  AI can generate pieces of code in HTML, CSS, and JavaScript based on a descriptive prompt. For example, if you need a responsive navigation bar, you can simply ask the AI, "Create a responsive navigation bar with a dropdown menu," and it will provide you with the corresponding code.

- **Error Detection and Correction:**
  Modern AI tools can scan your code for errors and suggest corrections, helping you learn best practices while fixing mistakes in real time.

- **Design Suggestions:**
  Some AI platforms offer visual design improvements. They can suggest color schemes, layout adjustments, and even animations, making your website more attractive without deep design knowledge.

Real-World Example:
Imagine you want to build a landing page for a new product. Instead of writing code from scratch, you can instruct your AI assistant with a prompt like, "Generate an HTML structure for a landing page with a hero section, features area, and contact form." The AI then provides you with a scaffold that you can customize. This not only saves time but also gives you a practical learning experience.

Exercise 1:

- **Task:** Use your AI assistant to generate code for a simple web page that contains a header, a paragraph, and a button.

- **Steps:**

  1. Open your preferred online code editor (e.g., CodePen, Replit, or JSFiddle).

  2. Type a prompt such as, "Generate a simple HTML page with a header that says 'Welcome', a paragraph of text, and a clickable button labeled 'Learn More'."

  3. Review the output and try to identify how the code is structured.

- **Action Item:** Customize the code by changing the button text and adjusting the styling with CSS.

41

Checklist for AI Code Generation:

- Write a clear and concise prompt for the AI.

- Verify that the generated code contains proper HTML, CSS, and JavaScript if applicable.

- Test the code by running it in an online editor.

- Modify the code to personalize it further.

Section 2: How to Ask AI the Right Questions

The quality of the code and suggestions you receive from an AI assistant depends largely on how you ask your questions. Learning the art of effective prompt formulation is essential.

2.1 Crafting Effective Prompts

- **Be Specific:**
  The more specific you are, the better your results will be. Instead of asking, "Create a webpage," try asking, "Generate an HTML page with a centered header, a paragraph with placeholder text, and a button that changes color on hover."

- **Break Down Complex Requests:**
  When dealing with multi-step tasks, divide your prompt into parts. Ask for one feature at a time (e.g., first generate the HTML structure, then ask for CSS styling, and finally request JavaScript interactivity).

- **Provide Context:**
  Let the AI know the purpose or context of your request. For example, "I am building a portfolio website for photography. Create a section to display images in a grid layout."

2.2 Common Prompt Pitfalls and How to Avoid Them

- **Vague Instructions:**
  Avoid general questions that leave too much room for interpretation. Always add details about what you want to see.

- **Overloading Requests:**
  Asking for too many details in one prompt may confuse the AI. Instead, keep each request focused on a single aspect.

- **Ignoring Feedback:**
  If the AI-generated output isn't quite right, refine your prompt. Experiment with rephrasing until you achieve the desired result.

Real-World Example:
Suppose you need a code snippet for a responsive image gallery. A less effective prompt might be, "Make an image gallery." A more effective one would be, "Generate an HTML and CSS code snippet for a responsive image gallery with three columns on desktop and one column on mobile devices."

Exercise 2:

- **Task:** Practice rewriting vague prompts into clear, detailed instructions.

- **Steps:**

  1. Write down a vague prompt, e.g., "Make a contact form."

  2. Revise it into a more detailed prompt, e.g., "Generate HTML and CSS code for a contact form that includes fields for name, email, and message, with a submit button that highlights on hover."

  3. Compare the results using your AI assistant.

- **Action Item:** Keep a journal of your prompts and the outputs. Note what changes led to better results.

Checklist for Asking Effective AI Questions:

- Identify the specific feature you need.

- Break down the feature into manageable parts.

- Include necessary details such as layout, styling, and interactivity.

- Experiment and adjust based on the AI's feedback.

Section 3: What AI Can (and Can't) Do for You

While AI is a powerful tool for website building, it's important to understand its strengths and limitations.

3.1 What AI Can Do

- **Generate Boilerplate Code:**
  AI excels at generating the initial code scaffold for a project. This includes setting up basic HTML structures and CSS styling that you can then customize.

- **Offer Code Suggestions and Best Practices:**
  Many AI systems are programmed with industry standards, meaning they can recommend improvements and corrections to your code.

- **Streamline Routine Tasks:**
  Tasks such as creating repetitive elements (e.g., buttons, forms) or generating consistent design patterns can be automated, allowing you to focus on creative and unique aspects of your project.

- **Provide Learning Assistance:**
  As you see code generated by AI, it reinforces your learning by showing you examples of good coding practices and logical structure.

3.2 What AI Can't Do

- **Replace Human Creativity and Critical Thinking:**
  Although AI can provide a great starting point, it doesn't fully understand your unique vision. Customization and creative decision-making remain in your hands.

- **Solve Highly Complex or Unique Problems:**
  For advanced functionalities or highly specific use cases, AI might generate generic code that requires significant tweaking by a human developer.

- **Understand Context Without Guidance:**
  AI works best when given clear and specific instructions. Without proper context, it may not deliver what you envisioned.

Real-World Example:
Consider the task of building an entire e-commerce website with tailored features like secure payment integration and advanced inventory management. AI can help create the layout and basic functionalities, but you will need to adjust and enhance the code to ensure it meets the unique needs of your business and security standards.

Exercise 3:

- **Task:** Identify a website feature that you'd like to build, and list what aspects you expect AI to handle versus what you will need to customize manually.

- **Steps:**

  1. Choose a feature, such as an interactive portfolio slider.

  2. Write down the parts of the feature that AI can generate (e.g., HTML structure, basic CSS styling).

  3. List the parts that will require your personal touch (e.g., personalized animations, unique design elements).

- **Action Item:** Create a plan for your next project that outlines which features can be sourced from AI assistance and which require custom coding.

Checklist for Understanding AI Capabilities:

- Recognize the types of code AI can generate reliably.

- Identify areas where human expertise and creativity are required.

- Test AI-generated code and compare it with your vision.

- Adjust and refine the code manually as needed.

Summary

In Chapter 3, you've met your AI Website Builder Assistant and learned how to leverage AI to streamline your coding process. We explored:

- **How AI Can Help Write Website Code:**
  From generating boilerplate code to suggesting design improvements, AI is an excellent ally for beginners.

- **How to Ask AI the Right Questions:**
  Crafting clear, specific prompts is key to getting the best output from your AI assistant.

- **What AI Can (and Can't) Do for You:**
  While AI makes many tasks easier, it also has its limits — your creativity and critical thinking remain essential.

As you practice with these exercises and action items, you'll grow increasingly confident in using AI to enhance your web development skills. Remember, using AI is about collaboration: it provides guidance and efficiency, while you infuse creativity and personalization into your projects.

Chapter 4: How to Ask AI for HTML Code

In this chapter, you'll learn how to effectively use AI to generate HTML code. We'll cover how to create structure with headings, paragraphs, images, and links, craft simple prompts that yield great results, and combine multiple elements to build a complete web page. With clear explanations, real-world examples, and plenty of exercises, you'll gain the confidence to harness AI as your web development assistant.

Learning Objectives

By the end of this chapter, you will be able to:

- **Create the Basic Structure of a Web Page:**

    - Understand how to use HTML elements such as headings, paragraphs, images, and links.

- **Formulate Effective Prompts for AI:**

    - Write simple yet detailed prompts to generate accurate HTML code.

    - Recognize key details that help guide the AI for better output.

- **Combine Multiple HTML Elements into a Single Page:**

    - Assemble various components into a coherent layout.

- Learn strategies to organize and refine AI-generated code.

- **Practice and Verify Your Code:**

    - Engage in hands-on exercises, sample prompts, and action items.

    - Use checklists to track your progress and reinforce key concepts.

Section 1: Creating Structure with HTML Elements

HTML is the foundation of every web page. It defines the content's structure using elements like headings, paragraphs, images, and links. Let's break down each of these components.

1.1 Headings and Paragraphs

Explanation:

- **Headings:**
  HTML provides six levels of headings, from <h1> (the most important) to <h6> (the least important). Headings help organize content and improve readability.

- **Paragraphs:**
  Paragraphs are created with the <p> tag. They are used for blocks of text and create a clear separation of ideas.

Real-World Example:
Imagine a blog post on travel adventures. You could use `<h1>` for the title, `<h2>` for section headings like "Destinations" or "Travel Tips," and `<p>` for the main body text.

Exercise:

- **Task:** Write HTML code for a blog post title and an introductory paragraph.

- **Steps:**

    1. Open your code editor.

    2. Write a snippet using `<h1>` for the title and `<p>` for the introduction.

- **Action Item:** Experiment by adding `<h2>` and `<h3>` headers for sub-sections.

Checklist:

- Create a `<h1>` element for your title.

- Write a `<p>` element for the introductory paragraph.

- Include additional headings to structure your content.

1.2 Adding Images

Explanation:
Images enhance visual appeal and support your content. Use the `<img>` tag to add images to your web page. Remember to include the `src` attribute (linking to the image) and the `alt` attribute (a text description for accessibility).

Real-World Example:
For a travel blog, include images of destinations. For example, use an `<img>` tag to show a photo of a famous landmark.

Exercise:

- **Task:** Insert an image into your HTML.

- **Steps:**

  1. Choose an image URL (or use a placeholder image service).

  2. Write the `<img>` tag with appropriate `src` and `alt` attributes.

- **Action Item:** Adjust the image size using inline CSS or by linking to an external stylesheet.

Checklist:

- Include an `<img>` tag.

- Specify a valid `src` URL.

- Add an `alt` attribute for accessibility.

1.3 Creating Hyperlinks

Explanation:
Hyperlinks enable navigation between web pages and other resources. Use the <a> tag to create links, and include the href attribute to define the destination URL.

Real-World Example:
In a personal portfolio, use hyperlinks to connect to your social media profiles, blogs, or other relevant sites.

Exercise:

- **Task:** Create a hyperlink that directs users to your favorite website.

- **Steps:**

    1. Write the <a> tag.

    2. Set the href attribute to the desired URL.

    3. Place text within the tag that describes the link.

- **Action Item:** Experiment with opening the link in a new tab by adding target="_blank" to your <a> tag.

Checklist:

- Create an <a> tag with a valid href value.

- Include descriptive link text.

- Optionally add target="_blank" for a new window/tab.

Section 2: Simple Prompts That Give Great Results

To get the most out of your AI assistant, it is essential to know how to formulate clear and specific prompts. Here's how:

2.1 Basic Prompt Structure

Guidelines:

- **Be Clear and Concise:**
  Instead of writing, "Give me some HTML code," specify, "Generate HTML code for a webpage with a heading, a paragraph, and an image."

- **Include Required Elements:**
  Mention all the HTML elements you want the AI to generate, such as headers, paragraphs, images, and links.

- **Provide Context:**
  For example, "Create a simple landing page with a welcome message, a brief description, and a link to learn more."

Real-World Example:
Prompt:

> "Generate HTML code for a basic webpage that includes a main heading, a paragraph describing the site, an image banner at the top, and a hyperlink to an external resource."

This detailed prompt sets clear expectations, resulting in a structured output that you can easily build upon.

2.2 Tips for Successful Prompts

- **Test and Refine:**
  If the output isn't perfect, slightly modify your prompt and try again.

- **Step-by-Step Prompts:**
  Break down complex pages into smaller sections. Generate one part at a time (e.g., first ask for the header structure, then the body content).

- **Use Examples in Prompts:**
  Including a sample phrase, such as "a header saying 'Welcome to My Site'" helps steer the AI.

Exercise:

- **Task:** Practice writing and testing different prompts.

- **Steps:**

    1. Write one prompt for a header and paragraph.

    2. Write another for an image with specific attributes.

    3. Compare the AI outputs and adjust your prompts as needed.

- **Action Item:** Keep a record of prompts that produce the best results for future reference.

Checklist for Prompt Creation:

- Provide a clear and detailed description.

- Specify all required elements.

- Include context or sample text.

- Test the prompt and refine if necessary.

Section 3: Combining Multiple Elements into a Page

Once you have mastered individual elements, it's time to bring them together to create a complete web page.

3.1 Building a Complete Web Page

Combining headings, paragraphs, images, and links is similar to assembling a puzzle. Each component has its own role, and together they form the final design.

Step-by-Step Example:

HTML Structure:

```
<!DOCTYPE html>
<html>
<head>
    <title>My AI-Generated Web Page</title>
    <link rel="stylesheet"
href="styles.css">
</head>
<body>
    <!-- Header Section -->
    <header>
        <h1>Welcome to My Website</h1>
        <p>This website is built using AI-
generated HTML code.</p>
    </header>
```

```
<!-- Image Section -->
<section>
    <img
src="https://via.placeholder.com/800x300"
alt="Banner Image">
    </section>
    <!-- Content Section -->
    <section>
        <h2>About This Site</h2>
        <p>This page demonstrates how AI can
help you write HTML code, combining multiple
elements into a cohesive layout.</p>
        <a href="https://example.com"
target="_blank">Learn More</a>
    </section>
</body>
</html>
```

1. **Explanation:**

   o The `<header>` contains a main heading and a
     paragraph.

   o An `<img>` element is used to show a banner
     image.

   o Another `<section>` includes additional
     content with a subheading, paragraph, and a
     hyperlink.

Real-World Example:
Consider an online portfolio where your homepage
introduces you, displays a professional image, and provides
navigation to your projects. This example HTML structure is
a foundation that you can expand with more sections as
needed.

3.2 Exercise: Build Your Own Page

- **Task:** Create a simple web page that combines a header, an image, a text section, and a link.

- **Steps:**

    1. Write the HTML structure using the example above as guidance.

    2. Customize the text, image URL, and link to reflect your personal style.

    3. Save your work and open the file in your browser to see the result.

- **Action Item:** Experiment with rearranging the elements. Try adding another section, such as a footer, with additional information like contact details or social media links.

Checklist for Combining Elements:

- Create a clear HTML structure with `<html>`, `<head>`, and `<body>` tags.

- Include at least one heading, paragraph, image, and hyperlink.

- Verify that each section is logically separated (e.g., using `<header>`, `<section>`, `<footer>`).

- Test the complete page in a browser to ensure it displays correctly.

Summary

In Chapter 4, you learned how to ask AI for HTML code and combine various elements to create a fully structured web page. You explored:

- **Creating Structure:**
  How to use headings, paragraphs, images, and links to build the content of your page.

- **Writing Effective Prompts:**
  Strategies for crafting clear, detailed prompts that deliver the code you need.

- **Integrating Multiple Elements:**
  Techniques for assembling individual components into a cohesive, complete web page.

By practicing the exercises, action items, and checklists throughout this chapter, you'll become more adept at using AI to generate HTML code. This skill not only speeds up your website development process but also builds your confidence to take on more complex projects.

Keep experimenting with different prompts and customization options, and enjoy the journey as you build your own web pages with the help of your AI assistant. Happy coding!

Chapter 5: How to Ask AI for CSS Styling

Welcome to Chapter 5, where we dive into the exciting world of CSS styling with the help of AI. In this chapter, you'll learn how to use AI to generate and refine CSS code so you can change colors, fonts, and layouts; make your page look attractive without the stress; and get creative with backgrounds, hover effects, and borders. Whether you want to give your website a polished look or experiment with unique designs, this guide will show you how to work with AI to achieve your styling goals.

Learning Objectives

By the end of this chapter, you will be able to:

- **Understand the Fundamentals of CSS Styling:**

    - Change colors, fonts, and layouts using CSS.

    - Recognize how these style changes affect the overall look of your webpage.

- **Ask AI for CSS Styling Help Effectively:**

    - Craft clear, detailed prompts that yield accurate and creative CSS outputs.

    - Identify specific styling needs and communicate them to your AI assistant.

- **Apply Advanced CSS Techniques with AI:**

- Create creative backgrounds, hover effects, and borders.

- Customize your webpage's visual elements to achieve a unique design.

- **Practice and Enhance Your Styling Skills:**

  - Engage in exercises and practice activities that reinforce your understanding.

  - Use checklists and action items to ensure a structured approach toward mastering CSS styling.

Section 1: Changing Colors, Fonts, and Layouts

CSS (Cascading Style Sheets) is the language of style for web pages. It controls the way HTML elements look on the screen — from colors and fonts to positioning and spacing. Let's begin by exploring some of the core properties that every beginner should know.

1.1 Changing Colors

Explanation:

- To change the color of text, use the `color` property.

- To change the background color of an element, use the `background-color` property.

Real-World Example:
Suppose you have a webpage with a title and a paragraph, and you want to make the title blue and the background of the paragraph light gray. You can ask your AI for a code snippet like:

> "Generate CSS that sets the title color to blue and the paragraph background to light gray."

Code Example:

```
h1 {
    color: blue;
}
p {
    background-color: #f2f2f2;
}
```

1.2 Changing Fonts

Explanation:

- Change fonts using the `font-family` property.

- You can also control the size, weight, and style with properties like `font-size`, `font-weight`, and `font-style`.

Real-World Example:
If you want your body text to be in Arial and your headings in Georgia, you could instruct the AI:

> "Generate CSS code that sets the body font to Arial, sans-serif, and the headings to Georgia, serif."

Code Example:

```css
body {
    font-family: Arial, sans-serif;
}
h1, h2, h3 {
    font-family: Georgia, serif;
}
```

1.3 Adjusting Layouts

Explanation:
CSS layouts help arrange elements on a webpage. Some key properties include `margin`, `padding`, `display`, and `flexbox` settings.

Real-World Example:
You might want to center a container on the page with some padding for spacing. Ask the AI:

> "Generate CSS for a container that is centered on the page with a width of 80%, margin auto, and 20px of padding."

Code Example:

```css
.container {
    width: 80%;
    margin: 0 auto;
    padding: 20px;
}
```

Checklist for Basic CSS Styling:

- Specify text and background colors.

- Choose appropriate font families for different text elements.

- Use margin and padding to adjust spacing.

- Experiment with layout properties to arrange elements.

Section 2: Making Your Page Look Good (Without Stress)

Creating a visually appealing webpage can seem daunting, but AI can help simplify the process. Let's discuss how to use AI to make style decisions and streamline your design workflow.

2.1 Simplified Styling with AI Prompts

Explanation:
AI can provide you with a starting point for your CSS code that looks professional and modern. By providing clear prompts, you can obtain styles that automatically adjust aspects like color schemes, font selections, and responsive layouts.

Real-World Example:
Imagine you're designing a portfolio page. You might ask the AI:

> "Generate CSS that gives my portfolio a modern, minimalist style with a neutral color palette and smooth margins."

Action Item:
Experiment with different prompts. Start simple — like changing the color of text or setting a background — and gradually ask for more complex layouts as you become comfortable.

2.2 Stress-Free Design Tips

- **Use Consistent Color Schemes:**
  Ask AI to suggest harmonious color schemes based on color theory.

- **Keep It Simple:**
  A minimalist design often looks more professional. Ask for CSS that emphasizes clean lines and ample whitespace.

- **Utilize CSS Frameworks:**
  Consider asking the AI for references to popular frameworks like Bootstrap or Tailwind CSS for additional inspiration.

Exercise:

- **Task:** Write a prompt for the AI that specifies a complete style for a simple web page, including a header, body, and footer.

- **Steps:**

    1. Define your color palette.

    2. Specify the fonts for headings and paragraphs.

    3. Request a layout for a centered container.

- **Action Item:** Use the generated CSS and incorporate it into your project. Adjust settings until it meets your visual preferences.

Checklist for Stress-Free Styling:

- Develop a clear idea of the design aesthetic.

- Use AI to generate starting CSS code.

- Modify the code to personalize colors, fonts, and layouts.

- Test the styles on your webpage to ensure a cohesive look.

Section 3: Getting Creative: Backgrounds, Hover Effects, Borders

Now that you understand the basics, let's explore some creative techniques to make your website stand out.

3.1 Custom Backgrounds

Explanation:
Backgrounds can dramatically alter the mood of your webpage. You can use images, gradients, or solid colors.

Real-World Example:
Ask the AI:

> "Generate CSS code for a section with a background image overlaid with a semi-transparent gradient."

Code Example:

```
.section-background {
    background: linear-gradient(rgba(0, 0,
0, 0.5), rgba(0, 0, 0, 0.5)),

url('https://via.placeholder.com/1200x400')
no-repeat center center;
    background-size: cover;
}
```

3.2 Hover Effects

Explanation:
Hover effects are a great way to add interactivity to your page. They can be applied to buttons, links, images, and more.

Real-World Example:
Consider a button that changes its background color when the user hovers over it. You can ask AI:

> "Generate CSS for a button that changes from blue to green on hover."

Code Example:

```css
.button {
    background-color: blue;
    color: white;
    padding: 10px 20px;
    border: none;
    cursor: pointer;
    transition: background-color 0.3s ease;
}
.button:hover {
    background-color: green;
}
```

3.3 Creative Borders

Explanation:
Borders can be used to frame elements and add a creative touch. You can customize their color, thickness, style (solid, dashed, dotted), and even add rounded corners.

Real-World Example:
For example, a card element on your page can have a soft, rounded border. Ask the AI:

"Generate CSS for a card with a 2px solid gray border and 10px border-radius."

Code Example:

```css
.card {
    border: 2px solid gray;
    border-radius: 10px;
    padding: 20px;
    box-shadow: 2px 2px 5px rgba(0, 0, 0,
0.1);
}
```

Checklist for Creative CSS Styling:

- Experiment with background images and gradients.

- Add hover effects to buttons and links.

- Customize borders and corners to enhance visual appeal.

- Test creative styles on various elements of your webpage.

Summary and Action Items

In Chapter 5, you learned how to ask AI for CSS styling to transform your website into a visually compelling project. You explored:

- **Changing Colors, Fonts, and Layouts:**
  How to control basic style properties to set the tone of your webpage.

- **Making Your Page Look Good (Without Stress):** Simplifying design decisions with AI-generated code and employing easy-to-follow prompts.

- **Getting Creative with CSS:** Using advanced techniques like custom backgrounds, hover effects, and borders to add flair and interactivity.

Action Items to Practice What You've Learned:

1. **Basic Styling Challenge:**

   - Create a simple webpage that uses different text colors and fonts.

   - Experiment with margins and padding to adjust the layout.

   - Use a checklist to ensure you have included all basic style elements.

2. **Advanced Effects Challenge:**

   - Ask the AI for CSS code to create a button with a dynamic hover effect.

   - Incorporate a background image with a gradient overlay in one section of your page.

   - Customize a card element with creative borders and a subtle shadow.

3. **Personalization Task:**

- Reflect on the visual style you'd like for your website and write a clear prompt for the AI.

- Combine the AI output with your custom tweaks to create a cohesive design.

- Save, test, and iterate on your design to develop your unique visual identity.

Remember, the key to mastering CSS styling is to experiment and refine. Use these exercises and checklists as stepping stones on your journey toward creating beautiful, professional websites with the help of AI. Enjoy the process, and don't be afraid to get creative!

Chapter 6: How to Ask AI for Simple JavaScript

In this chapter, you'll learn how to harness AI to add interactivity to your web pages using JavaScript. We'll explore how to generate basic JavaScript code to create interactive buttons, display alerts, and perform form validation. Moreover, you'll discover how to describe the specific behaviors you want, whether it's making your page do something fun or adding essential functionality.

Learning Objectives

By the end of this chapter, you will be able to:

- **Understand the Role of JavaScript in Web Development:**

    o Learn how JavaScript enhances user interactivity on web pages.

    o Recognize common use cases such as buttons, alerts, and form validations.

- **Ask AI for JavaScript Code Effectively:**

    o Write simple, clear prompts to generate JavaScript code.

    o Break down behavior requests into manageable parts for the AI.

- **Implement Basic JavaScript Interactions:**

- Add interactive buttons that trigger alerts or other actions.

- Create simple form validation to improve user experience.

- Experiment with fun and creative JavaScript behaviors.

- **Practice and Reinforce Your Skills:**

  - Engage with real-world examples, exercises, and action items.

  - Use checklists to track progress and ensure you incorporate key concepts.

Section 1: Adding Interactivity with JavaScript

JavaScript is the engine that powers interactive elements on your web page. While HTML structures your content and CSS styles it, JavaScript makes your page come alive — responding to user actions like button clicks, displaying alerts, and validating forms.

1.1 Buttons and Alerts

Explanation:
Buttons are one of the most common interactive elements on a page, and they can trigger a variety of actions. One simple action is displaying an alert box when a button is clicked.

Real-World Example:

Imagine a "Click Me" button on a welcome page. When clicked, it might display an alert saying, "Welcome to my website!"

Simple Code Example:

```
<!DOCTYPE html>
<html>
<head>
    <title>JavaScript Example - Alert
Button</title>
</head>
<body>
    <button id="alertButton">Click
Me!</button>
    <script>
        const alertButton =
document.getElementById('alertButton');

alertButton.addEventListener('click',
function() {
            alert('Welcome to my website!');
        });
    </script>
</body>
</html>
```

Exercise:

1. Open your code editor and create a new HTML file.

2. Copy the code above into your file.

3. Save and open the file in your browser.

4. Click the button and observe the alert.

Action Item: Try changing the alert message to something personal or fun. Note down your changes and see how different messages make you feel about the interaction.

Checklist for Buttons and Alerts:

- Create a button element with a unique ID.

- Write JavaScript to select the button.

- Attach an event listener to the button for a click event.

- Display an alert message when clicked.

Section 2: Simple Form Validation

Form validation is a common use of JavaScript. It ensures that users enter data correctly before submitting a form. This can include checking if fields are not empty, if an email address is correctly formatted, or if passwords meet specific criteria.

2.1 Describing Basic Form Behavior

Explanation:
A simple form might ask for a user's name and email. JavaScript can verify that both fields are filled out and alert the user if something is missing.

Real-World Example:
Imagine a newsletter subscription form. When the user clicks "Submit," JavaScript checks if both the name and email are provided. If not, it displays an alert asking the user to complete the missing fields.

Simple Code Example:

```
<!DOCTYPE html>
<html>
<head>
    <title>Simple Form Validation</title>
</head>
<body>
    <form id="subscriptionForm">
        <label for="name">Name:</label>
        <input type="text" id="name"
name="name"><br><br>
        <label for="email">Email:</label>
        <input type="email" id="email"
name="email"><br><br>
        <button
type="submit">Submit</button>
    </form>
    <script>
        const form =
document.getElementById('subscriptionForm');
        form.addEventListener('submit',
function(event) {
            // Prevent form submission to
check data first
            event.preventDefault();
            const name =
document.getElementById('name').value;
            const email =
document.getElementById('email').value;
            if (name === '' || email === '')
{
                alert('Please fill in both
your name and email.');
            } else {
```

```
                alert('Thank you for
subscribing!');
                // Here, you might normally
submit the form or process the data.
            }
        });
    </script>
</body>
</html>
```

Exercise:

1. Create a new HTML file with the sample form validation code above.

2. Test the form by submitting it with one or both fields empty.

3. Verify that the alert appears as expected and then try it with both fields filled.

Action Item: Modify the form to include an additional field (e.g., phone number) and update the validation logic accordingly.

Checklist for Form Validation:

- Build a simple HTML form with required fields.

- Attach an event listener to handle form submission.

- Write JavaScript to check for empty fields.

- Display appropriate alerts based on the input data.

Section 3: Making Your Page Do Something Fun

Beyond essential interactions, JavaScript can make your page engaging and fun. Whether it's a dynamic image gallery, a moving animation, or playful text changes, the possibilities are endless.

3.1 Describing Fun Behaviors to AI

Explanation:
To ask AI for code that adds a playful element, clearly describe what you want. For example, "Generate JavaScript that changes the background color every time a user clicks a button" is a detailed prompt that specifies both the action (click) and the behavior (background color change).

Real-World Example:
Create a fun button that, when clicked, cycles the background color of the page through a set of colors.

Prompt Example for AI:

"Generate JavaScript code for a button that cycles the webpage background color through red, blue, and green each time it is clicked."

Sample Code Generated Could Look Like:

```
<!DOCTYPE html>
<html>
<head>
    <title>Fun Background Color
Change</title>
</head>
<body>
    <button id="colorCycleButton">Change
Background Color</button>
```

```
<script>
      const colorCycleButton =
document.getElementById('colorCycleButton');
      const colors = ['red', 'blue',
'green'];
      let colorIndex = 0;

colorCycleButton.addEventListener('click',
function() {

document.body.style.backgroundColor =
colors[colorIndex];
            colorIndex = (colorIndex + 1) %
colors.length;
      });
   </script>
</body>
</html>
```

Exercise:

1. Create a new HTML file and paste the code above.

2. Open the file in your browser and click the button to see the background color change.

3. Experiment by adding more colors to the array and see how the changes affect the cycling pattern.

Action Item: Develop a creative prompt for your own interactive feature, such as making text change or adding an animation effect. Test the output and tweak the code to match your vision.

Checklist for Fun Interactivity:

- Clearly describe the behavior you want in your AI prompt.

- Generate and test JavaScript code that implements the behavior.

- Experiment with modifications to personalize the fun effect.

- Ensure the interactivity works smoothly in your browser.

Summary and Final Practice

In Chapter 6, you learned how to ask AI for simple JavaScript code to bring interactivity to your website. We covered:

- **Adding Basic Interactivity:**
  How to implement buttons and alerts to make your page respond to user actions.

- **Form Validation:**
  Techniques for using JavaScript to check user input and ensure proper form submission.

- **Fun and Engaging Interactions:**
  Methods to create playful behaviors like cycling background colors or triggering animations, enhancing the user experience.

Final Action Items

1. **Interactive Buttons Project:**

- Create an HTML page with two buttons: one that displays an alert and another that changes an element's text.

- Modify the code to add different behaviors for each button.

2. **Complete Form Validation:**

   - Build a form with multiple fields (name, email, and a phone number), and implement JavaScript to validate that all fields are filled.

   - Adjust the validation messages to make them fun and friendly.

3. **Fun Feature Challenge:**

   - Use your creativity to generate a JavaScript feature, such as a color-changing background or moving elements.

   - Write a clear prompt for the AI to get started and customize the code as needed.

Checklist for Mastering Simple JavaScript:

- Understand the purpose of JavaScript on a webpage.

- Write effective AI prompts that describe desired behaviors.

- Implement basic interactions such as alerts and form validation.

- Experiment with creative, fun JavaScript effects.

- Test your code in a browser and refine based on feedback.

By practicing these exercises and following the action items, you'll gain confidence in using AI to write simple JavaScript. Your web pages will not only look great but also engage your users with interactive features. Enjoy experimenting with code and exploring the creative possibilities that JavaScript—and AI—offer!

Chapter 7: Building a Basic Web Page

Welcome to Chapter 7! In this chapter, you will learn how to build your very first web page from scratch. We will walk through creating the basic HTML skeleton, adding text, images, and links, and finally testing your page in a web browser. This chapter is designed to be beginner-friendly and self-contained so that you can follow along without any prior knowledge of web development.

Learning Objectives

By the end of this chapter, you will be able to:

- **Create an HTML Skeleton:**

    - Understand the structure of an HTML document including the `<html>`, `<head>`, and `<body>` elements.

- **Add Content to Your Web Page:**

    - Use HTML tags to add text elements such as headings and paragraphs.

    - Insert images using the `<img>` tag.

    - Create hyperlinks with the `<a>` tag to link to external websites or other pages.

- **Test Your Web Page in a Browser:**

    - Learn how to open your HTML file in a web browser.

- Verify that your code displays correctly and troubleshoot common issues.

- **Practice and Enhance Your Skills:**

  - Participate in hands-on exercises and practice activities.

  - Follow action items and checklists that keep you on track as you build your first web page.

Section 1: Your First HTML Skeleton

An HTML skeleton is the basic structure of any web page. It sets up the framework that you will then fill with content.

Explanation

An HTML document begins with the `<!DOCTYPE html>` declaration, which tells the browser what version of HTML you're using. After that, the document is wrapped in `<html>` tags. Inside the `<html>` element, you have two main sections:

- **`<head>` Element:**
  This contains metadata about your page, like its title, character set, links to external stylesheets, and more.

- **`<body>` Element:**
  This is where the content that appears on your page goes. All text, images, and links will be placed here.

Example: HTML Skeleton

Below is an example of a simple HTML skeleton:

```
<!DOCTYPE html>
<html>
<head>
    <meta charset="UTF-8">
    <title>My First Web Page</title>
</head>
<body>
    <!-- Your content goes here -->
    <h1>Welcome to My Website!</h1>
    <p>This is my very first web page built
with HTML.</p>
</body>
</html>
```

Exercise 1: Create Your HTML Skeleton

1. Open your favorite text editor or an online editor
   (like CodePen, Replit, or JSFiddle).

2. Create a new file and save it as `index.html`.

3. Type in the code above to create your HTML
   skeleton.

4. Save the file.

Action Item:
Print or write down the structure of your HTML document.
Identify the `<head>` and `<body>` sections and note what
each section will be used for in your future projects.

Checklist:

- Include the `<!DOCTYPE html>` declaration.

- Create `<html>`, `<head>`, and `<body>` tags.

84

- Add a `<meta charset="UTF-8">` tag in the `<head>`.

- Provide a title using the `<title>` tag.

Section 2: Adding Text, Images, and Links

Now that you have your basic HTML skeleton, it's time to fill it with content.

2.1 Adding Text

Explanation:
Text is added with various tags. The `<h1>` tag creates a large header, while `<p>` creates a paragraph for normal text.

Example:

```
<h1>Welcome to My Website!</h1>
<p>This is my first attempt at building a
web page. I am excited to learn more about
web development!</p>
```

2.2 Adding Images

Explanation:
Images are added using the `<img>` tag. You need to specify the `src` attribute (the image URL or path) and the `alt` attribute (a description of the image for accessibility).

Example:

```
<img src="https://via.placeholder.com/300"
alt="Placeholder Image">
```

2.3 Adding Hyperlinks

Explanation:

Hyperlinks let you link to other pages or websites. Use the <a> tag with the href attribute to define the destination URL.

Example:

```
<a href="https://www.example.com"
target="_blank">Visit Example.com</a>
```

Exercise 2: Enhance Your Web Page

1. Within your HTML file, add a section to include a header, a paragraph, an image, and a hyperlink.

2. Use the examples above to guide you.

3. Customize the text, image URL, and link text to reflect something personal or interesting to you.

4. Save your changes.

Action Item:

Review your code to ensure proper nesting of tags and that each tag is used correctly. Experiment with modifying the text and see how it appears in your browser.

Checklist for Adding Content:

- Add at least one <h1> header and one <p> paragraph.

- Insert an <img> tag with valid src and descriptive alt.

- Create an <a> tag with a working href link.

- Validate that all elements appear on your web page as expected.

Section 3: Testing in the Browser

Before considering your page complete, you need to test it to see if everything displays as intended.

Explanation

Testing your page in a web browser is simple:

1. **Save your HTML file:** Make sure you've saved your file with the .html extension.

2. **Open the file:** Locate the file in your file explorer/finder, right-click on it, and choose "Open With" and then select your web browser.

3. **Review the Layout:** Check that your text, images, and links display correctly. Click links and interact with the page to test functionality.

4. **Troubleshoot Common Errors:**

   o Ensure tags are properly closed.

   o Verify that all file paths (for images or linked documents) are correct.

   o Use the browser's developer tools (usually accessed by pressing F12 or right-clicking and selecting "Inspect") to identify any issues.

Exercise 3: Test and Refine Your Page

1. Open your `index.html` file in a web browser.

2. Review how the page renders.

3. Make any adjustments to spacing, text, or image sizes if needed.

4. Refresh your browser to see changes in action.

Action Item:
Create a short report on what worked well on your page and what you would like to improve. Use this report to guide further refinements on your page.

Checklist for Testing:

- Save your HTML file with the correct extension.

- Open the file in a browser and inspect the layout.

- Test all hyperlinks to ensure they work as expected.

- Use browser developer tools to check for errors.

Summary and Final Practice

In Chapter 7, you have built your very first web page by creating an HTML skeleton, adding various content such as text, images, and links, and finally testing your work in the browser. These steps form the foundation of web development, and mastering them is a key milestone on your journey to building more complex websites with the help of AI.

Final Action Items

1. **Complete Your Web Page:**

   o Ensure your `index.html` contains all the basic components: structure, text, images, and links.

   o Test your web page thoroughly in at least two different browsers.

2. **Document Your Learning:**

   o Write down any challenges you encountered and how you solved them.

   o Keep a checklist of the steps you followed for future reference.

3. **Experiment with Customization:**

   o Try modifying the layout by adding more sections like a footer or additional paragraphs.

   o Explore simple CSS styling to further enhance the appearance of your web page.

Final Checklist for Building Your Basic Web Page:

- Created a proper HTML skeleton with `<!DOCTYPE html>`, `<html>`, `<head>`, and `<body>` tags.

- Included key content elements: headers, paragraphs, images, and hyperlinks.

- Tested and verified the web page in multiple browsers.

- Documented improvements and areas for further practice.

By following these steps and action items, you will gain the confidence and skills necessary to build web pages from scratch. Continue to experiment and build upon what you've learned to further enhance your web development prowess.

Chapter 8: Making It Beautiful with CSS

In Chapter 8, we focus on transforming your basic web page into a visually appealing website using CSS. You'll learn how to incorporate CSS through style tags and external stylesheets, change colors, fonts, and layouts, and even use AI to generate a basic design for you. With clear explanations, real-world examples, hands-on exercises, and action items, you'll be well-equipped to enhance your website's design.

Learning Objectives

By the end of this chapter, you will be able to:

- **Incorporate CSS into Your Website:**

  - Understand the use of style tags and external stylesheets to apply CSS.

- **Customize Visual Elements:**

  - Change colors, fonts, and layouts to create an attractive design.

- **Leverage AI for Design Suggestions:**

  - Learn how to prompt AI to generate a basic design or theme for your site.

- **Practice and Iterate:**

  - Engage with exercises, action items, and checklists to reinforce your styling skills.

Section 1: Adding CSS to Your Web Page

There are several ways to include CSS in your HTML, each with its benefits. You can embed CSS directly within your HTML file using style tags or use external stylesheets to keep your code organized and reusable.

1.1 Using the Style Tag

Explanation:
The style tag allows you to add CSS code directly inside an HTML document. It's placed inside the <head> section of your HTML file.

Example:

```
<!DOCTYPE html>
<html>
<head>
    <meta charset="UTF-8">
    <title>Stylish Web Page</title>
    <style>
        body {
            background-color: #f0f0f0;
            font-family: 'Arial', sans-
serif;
        }
        h1 {
            color: #333;
        }
        p {
            color: #666;
        }
    </style>
</head>
<body>
    <h1>Welcome to My Stylish Site</h1>
```

```
<p>This page uses a style tag for its
CSS.</p>
</body>
</html>
```

1.2 Using External Stylesheets

Explanation:
External stylesheets keep your CSS separate from your HTML, making it easier to manage larger projects. You create a separate file (commonly named `styles.css`) and link it within your HTML file.

Example:

HTML File (index.html):

```
<!DOCTYPE html>
<html>
<head>
    <meta charset="UTF-8">
    <title>My Externally Styled Web
Page</title>
    <link rel="stylesheet"
href="styles.css">
</head>
<body>
    <h1>Welcome to My Website</h1>
    <p>This page links to an external
stylesheet.</p>
</body>
</html>
```

External CSS File (styles.css):

```
body {
    background-color: #e0f7fa;
    font-family: 'Verdana', sans-serif;
```

```
}
h1 {
    color: #006064;
}
p {
    color: #004d40;
}
```

Exercise 1: Practice Adding CSS

Task:
Create an HTML file with a basic structure and include CSS using both a style tag and an external stylesheet.

Steps:

1. Create a file named `index.html` and add an HTML skeleton.

2. Add a style tag in the `<head>` and write a simple style for the body, header, and paragraph.

3. Create a separate file named `styles.css` and link it to your HTML file. Experiment with changing the background color and font.

Action Item:
Document which method you prefer and why. Note any challenges you encounter and how you resolved them.

Checklist:

- Create an HTML file with a proper `<head>` and `<body>`.

- Include a style tag with basic CSS.

- Create and link an external CSS file.

- Verify that the styles are applied correctly in your browser.

Section 2: Changing Colors, Fonts, and Layouts

Customizing the appearance of your webpage is crucial to creating an engaging user experience. With CSS, you can alter the visual aspects of your website to match the style and tone you want.

2.1 Changing Colors and Fonts

Explanation:
CSS properties such as `color` and `font-family` allow you to modify the appearance of text and backgrounds.

Example:

```
body {
    background-color: #fffbe6;
    font-family: 'Georgia', serif;
}
h1 {
    color: #b71c1c;
}
p {
    color: #4e342e;
}
```

Real-World Example:
For a personal blog, you might choose soft background colors with a mix of elegant fonts to give a warm and inviting feel. Use colors that are gentle on the eyes and fonts that enhance readability.

2.2 Adjusting Layouts

Explanation:
CSS properties like `margin`, `padding`, `display`, and `flexbox` help organize your content on the page. You can center content, create multi-column layouts, or add space between elements to improve readability.

Example:

```
.container {
    width: 80%;
    margin: 0 auto;
    padding: 20px;
    display: flex;
    flex-direction: column;
    align-items: center;
}
```

Real-World Example:
If you are designing a portfolio page, you may want to center your content and create spacing that allows each element to stand out. This approach helps create a clean, modern design.

Exercise 2: Customize Your Page's Style

Task:
Enhance your previously created web page by applying new CSS styles.

Steps:

1. Update your CSS to change the background color, text color, and font.

2. Use CSS layout properties to center your content and create extra space around elements.

3. Experiment with different values for margins and padding to observe their effects.

Action Item:
Write down at least three variations of your layout and choose the one that appeals to you the most.

Checklist:

- Change background colors and text colors.

- Set different font styles and sizes.

- Apply layout adjustments using margins and padding.

- Test each variation in your web browser.

Section 3: Using AI to Create a Basic Design for You

AI can serve as your creative partner when developing website designs. By providing clear prompts, you can have AI generate CSS code that follows modern design trends and best practices.

3.1 Writing Effective AI Prompts for CSS

Explanation:

A good prompt clearly describes the design you envision. It should include details about color schemes, font preferences, and layout structures.

Prompt Example:

"Generate CSS code for a modern, minimalist website with a white background, black header text, and gray body text. Include a centered container with 80% width, and use a clean sans-serif font for the body and a bold serif font for headers."

Real-World Example:

Imagine you want to create a landing page for a start-up. Your prompt can include specifics like a calm blue color scheme, spacious layout, and clearly defined sections. The AI returns a CSS snippet that you can tweak for your project.

3.2 Implementing AI-Generated CSS

Example AI-Generated Code:

```
body {
    background-color: #ffffff;
    font-family: 'Helvetica', sans-serif;
    color: #333333;
}
header {
    font-family: 'Times New Roman', serif;
    text-align: center;
    padding: 20px 0;
    background-color: #f5f5f5;
}
.container {
    width: 80%;
```

```
    margin: 0 auto;
    padding: 30px;
}
```

Exercise 3: Use AI to Generate a CSS Design

Task:

1. Write a detailed prompt for the AI that outlines your desired design attributes.

2. Copy the generated CSS code into your external stylesheet.

3. Refresh your web page to see the new design applied.

Action Item:
Refine the AI-generated code by incorporating your own customizations. Create a summary of what aspects of the design you liked and what you changed.

Checklist for Using AI-Generated Designs:

- Write a detailed and clear AI prompt.

- Copy the AI-generated CSS code into your stylesheet.

- Test the output in your browser.

- Personalize the design to better suit your preferences.

Summary and Final Practice

In Chapter 8, you have learned how to make your website look beautiful with CSS. You explored:

- **Different Methods to Include CSS:**
  How to use style tags within your HTML and link to external stylesheets for a cleaner, more organized codebase.

- **Changing Colors, Fonts, and Layouts:**
  The basic properties to transform the look and feel of your web page, ensuring that your design is both visually appealing and functional.

- **Leveraging AI for Design:**
  How to create detailed prompts to obtain AI-generated CSS code that can give you a polished starting point for your designs.

Final Action Items

1. **Complete Your Website's Design:**

   - Ensure your `index.html` is linked to a comprehensive `styles.css` file that includes all your styles.

   - Experiment with various color schemes, font choices, and layout adjustments until you're satisfied with the design.

2. **Document Your Process:**

   - Note down the prompts you wrote for the AI and the design changes you made.

   - Reflect on which techniques improved your website's appearance and how you might further refine your design in the future.

3. **Expand Your Design:**

   o Add at least one new section (such as a footer or an additional content section) and apply unique styling.

   o Test the responsiveness of your page, ensuring that the layout works on different screen sizes.

Final Checklist:

- Link your HTML file to a correctly formatted external stylesheet.

- Apply diverse CSS properties to change colors, fonts, and layouts.

- Generate design ideas with effective AI prompts and personalize the results.

- Test the final design in various browsers and screen sizes.

- Document your process and note improvements for future projects.

By following these instructions and practicing the exercises, you'll gain a solid understanding of CSS and learn to create beautiful, modern websites with the help of AI. As you continue experimenting and refining your design skills, you'll develop the confidence to build even more sophisticated projects.

Chapter 9: Making It Interactive with JavaScript

Welcome to Chapter 9! In this chapter, you will learn how to bring interactivity to your web pages using JavaScript. We will cover how to add buttons that respond to user actions, create a simple form that checks for proper input, and use AI to generate simple scripts to enhance your website's functionality. With clear explanations, real-world examples, hands-on exercises, and actionable checklists, you'll gain the skills you need to make your website dynamic and engaging.

Learning Objectives

By the end of this chapter, you will be able to:

- **Implement Interactive Buttons:**

    - Understand how to attach JavaScript events to buttons.

    - Create buttons that respond to user actions (e.g., displaying alerts or updating content).

- **Build a Simple Form with Input Validation:**

    - Learn how to create a form in HTML and enhance it with JavaScript validation.

    - Ensure that users provide the necessary input before submitting a form.

- **Utilize AI to Generate Easy JavaScript Scripts:**

- Write clear and effective prompts to ask AI for JavaScript snippets.

- Understand how to integrate AI-generated code into your projects.

- **Practice and Reinforce Your Skills:**

  - Engage with hands-on exercises and action items.

  - Use checklists to track your progress and verify that you have mastered each concept.

Section 1: Adding Buttons That Respond

Buttons are one of the simplest yet most powerful elements you can add to a web page. They allow users to trigger actions such as displaying messages, modifying content, or even navigating to other pages.

1.1 Explanation: Creating an Interactive Button

In JavaScript, you can add interactivity to a button by using event listeners. When a user clicks a button, an event is triggered. You can then define a function to execute when that event occurs.

Key Concepts:

- **Event Listener:** JavaScript code that waits for an event (like a click) to happen.

- **Callback Function:** A function that is executed when the event occurs.

1.2 Example: Button That Displays an Alert

Below is an example of an HTML file with a button that, when clicked, displays an alert message:

```
<!DOCTYPE html>
<html>
<head>
    <meta charset="UTF-8">
    <title>Interactive Button
Example</title>
</head>
<body>
    <button id="alertButton">Click
Me!</button>
    <script>
        // Select the button using its ID.
        const alertButton =
document.getElementById('alertButton');
        // Attach a click event listener to
the button.

alertButton.addEventListener('click',
function() {
            alert('Hello! You clicked the
button!');
        });
    </script>
</body>
</html>
```

Exercise 1: Create Your Own Interactive Button

1. Open your text editor and create a new HTML file named `interactive-button.html`.

2. Using the example above, modify the alert message to something personalized (for example, "Welcome to my interactive page!").

3. Save the file and open it in your browser. Click the button to ensure the alert works.

Action Item:
Write down what changes you made and note the steps you followed to attach the event listener.

Checklist:

- Create a button element with a unique ID.

- Use JavaScript to select the button.

- Attach a click event listener.

- Display an alert with a custom message when the button is clicked.

Section 2: Making a Simple Form That Checks for Input

Forms are essential for gathering user input. With JavaScript, you can verify that users fill out the necessary fields correctly before the form is processed.

2.1 Explanation: Basic Form Input Validation

Input validation ensures that users provide the required information and that it meets specified criteria (such as non-empty fields or correctly formatted emails). This helps prevent errors and improve the user experience.

Key Concepts:

- **Prevent Form Submission:** Using `event.preventDefault()` to stop the form from submitting if validation fails.

- **Accessing Form Data:** Retrieving values from input fields using JavaScript.

2.2 Example: Simple Form with Name and Email Validation

Below is a simple example of an HTML form that checks if the user has filled out both the "Name" and "Email" fields:

```html
<!DOCTYPE html>
<html>
<head>
    <meta charset="UTF-8">
    <title>Simple Form Validation</title>
</head>
<body>
    <form id="simpleForm">
        <label for="name">Name:</label>
        <input type="text" id="name"
name="name"><br><br>
        <label for="email">Email:</label>
        <input type="email" id="email"
name="email"><br><br>
        <button
type="submit">Submit</button>
    </form>
    <script>
        const form =
document.getElementById('simpleForm');
```

```
        form.addEventListener('submit',
function(event) {
            // Prevent the form from
submitting immediately
            event.preventDefault();
            // Retrieve the input values
            const nameValue =
document.getElementById('name').value;
            const emailValue =
document.getElementById('email').value;
            // Check if either field is
empty
            if (nameValue.trim() === '' ||
emailValue.trim() === '') {
                alert('Please fill in both
your name and email address.');
            } else {
                alert('Thank you for
submitting the form!');
                // Here, you might normally
submit the form data to a server.
            }
        });
    </script>
</body>
</html>
```

Exercise 2: Create a Validated Form

1. Create a new HTML file named form-
    validation.html.

2. Use the example above to build a form that collects a
    user's name and email.

3. Test the form in your browser by attempting to submit it with empty fields, then fill it out correctly to see the different responses.

Action Item:
Add an extra field (such as a phone number) and update the JavaScript validation to check that this field is also not empty.

Checklist:

- Create an HTML form with at least two input fields.

- Attach a submit event listener that prevents form submission if validation fails.

- Display alert messages to guide the user.

- Test the form with both valid and invalid inputs.

Section 3: Using AI to Help with Easy Scripts

AI tools can be incredibly helpful in generating JavaScript code snippets quickly. By providing clear instructions, you can have AI create code for interactive features, then tweak it as needed.

3.1 Writing Effective AI Prompts for JavaScript

Explanation:
An effective prompt for AI should include details about the desired functionality. For example, "Generate JavaScript code for a button that, when clicked, changes the text of a paragraph to 'Button Clicked!'" is clear and specific.

Tips for Writing Prompts:

- **Be Specific:** Mention exactly what action you want the button to perform.

- **Break Down the Task:** If your script involves multiple steps, ask for them one at a time.

- **Include Context:** Explain where the script will be used or any specific conditions.

3.2 Example: AI-Generated Script

Imagine you need a script for a button that updates the text inside a paragraph. You might use this prompt:

> "Generate JavaScript code for a button that, when clicked, changes the text of a paragraph with the ID 'message' to 'Button Clicked!'."

A possible AI-generated output could be:

```
<!DOCTYPE html>
<html>
<head>
    <meta charset="UTF-8">
    <title>AI Script Example</title>
</head>
<body>
    <p id="message">Original Text</p>
    <button id="updateButton">Click
Me!</button>
    <script>
        const updateButton =
document.getElementById('updateButton');
```

```
updateButton.addEventListener('click',
function() {

document.getElementById('message').textConte
nt = 'Button Clicked!';
        });
    </script>
</body>
</html>
```

Exercise 3: Use AI-Generated Code and Personalize It

1. Open your preferred AI coding tool or online editor that supports AI prompts.

2. Write a detailed prompt similar to the one above and generate the script.

3. Copy the generated code into a new HTML file named `ai-script.html`.

4. Modify the text or styling to better match your style.

Action Item:
Keep a log of different prompts you try and note how changes to your prompt affect the output. This will help you refine your prompt-writing skills.

Checklist for Using AI-Generated Scripts:

- Write a clear and specific prompt.

- Generate and review the AI-produced code.

- Integrate the generated code into your project.

- Personalize and test the final output.

Summary and Final Practice

In Chapter 9, you learned how to make your website interactive using JavaScript. You practiced:

- **Adding Interactive Buttons:**
  Learning to attach event listeners that trigger actions, such as displaying alerts.

- **Building a Simple Form with Input Validation:**
  Creating a form that checks for required input and responds with clear messages.

- **Using AI to Generate JavaScript Scripts:**
  Writing effective prompts to obtain quick, useful code from AI tools, then customizing it to fit your needs.

Final Action Items

1. **Build an Interactive Project:**

   ○ Create an HTML page that includes at least two interactive elements (e.g., a button that triggers an alert and a form that validates input).

   ○ Ensure that your page integrates clear messages and handles different user inputs gracefully.

2. **Document Your Process:**

- Write down the AI prompts you used and the modifications you made to the generated code.

- Create a checklist of the interactive elements implemented and any issues you encountered.

3. **Experiment and Iterate:**

   - Expand your project by adding a new interactive feature, such as changing the color of an element when clicked.

   - Test your new feature in different browsers to ensure consistent behavior.

Final Checklist:

- Implement buttons with click event listeners and custom alert messages.

- Create a form with validation that checks for empty fields.

- Use AI to generate simple scripts and modify them for your specific needs.

- Test all interactive features thoroughly in your browser.

- Document your work and refine your code based on user feedback.

By engaging with these exercises and action items, you've taken a significant step forward in making your website interactive with JavaScript. These skills not only enhance user engagement but also lay the groundwork for more complex programming tasks in the future.

Chapter 10: Mini Website Projects with AI

Welcome to Chapter 10! This chapter is where you bring everything together by working on mini website projects generated or enhanced with the help of AI. We will explore four distinct project types: a Personal Portfolio Page, a Simple Landing Page for a Product or Event, an Interactive Quiz Game Website, and a Photo Gallery with a Lightbox Effect. Each project will help you put your HTML, CSS, and JavaScript skills into practice while learning to communicate clearly with AI for code generation and design ideas.

Learning Objectives

By the end of this chapter, you will be able to:

- **Build Mini Website Projects:**

    - Create a Personal Portfolio Page to showcase your work.

    - Design a Simple Landing Page tailored for a product or event.

    - Develop an Interactive Quiz Game Website that engages users.

    - Assemble a Photo Gallery featuring a lightbox effect for viewing images.

- **Utilize AI Effectively:**

    - Write clear prompts to generate code snippets and design suggestions.

- Combine AI-generated code with your own customizations to produce complete projects.

- **Implement Key Web Technologies:**

  - Use HTML to structure your pages.

  - Apply CSS to enhance visual design and layout.

  - Integrate JavaScript for interactive functionalities.

- **Practice and Enhance Skills:**

  - Engage in hands-on exercises, sample projects, and action items.

  - Use checklists to track your progress through each mini project.

Section 1: Personal Portfolio Page

A personal portfolio website is an excellent way to showcase your skills, projects, and experiences. It serves as your digital resume, highlighting who you are and what you can do.

1.1 Explanation

Your portfolio page should include:

- **A Header:** Featuring your name or logo.

- **About Section:** A brief introduction and summary of your skills.

- **Projects Section:** Showcasing examples of your work.

- **Contact Information:** A way for visitors or potential employers to get in touch.

1.2 Example Structure

Here's a simple example of what the HTML structure for your portfolio might look like:

```
<!DOCTYPE html>
<html>
<head>
    <meta charset="UTF-8">
    <title>My Portfolio</title>
    <link rel="stylesheet"
href="portfolio.css">
</head>
<body>
    <header>
        <h1>Your Name</h1>
        <p>Web Developer & Designer</p>
    </header>
    <section id="about">
        <h2>About Me</h2>
        <p>A brief introduction about who
you are, your background, and your
skills.</p>
    </section>
    <section id="projects">
        <h2>My Projects</h2>
        <div class="project">
            <h3>Project Title</h3>
            <p>Short description of the
project...</p>
        </div>
```

```
    <!-- Additional projects can be
added here -->
    </section>
    <footer>
        <p>Contact: <a
href="mailto:yourname@example.com">yourname@
example.com</a></p>
    </footer>
</body>
</html>
```

1.3 Exercise and Action Items

- **Exercise:**

    ○ Create a file named `portfolio.html` and
      replicate the structure above.

    ○ Add your personal details and at least two
      projects.

    ○ Style the page using either an internal style tag
      or link to an external stylesheet
      (`portfolio.css`).

- **Action Items:**

    ○ Write a prompt for your AI tool such as:

        "Generate CSS for a modern, clean personal
        portfolio page with a centered header and
        responsive project cards."

- Customize the AI-generated code with your preferred colors and fonts.

- **Checklist:**

  - A header with your name and a tagline.

  - An About section with a brief self-introduction.

  - A Projects section showcasing at least two projects.

  - A footer with contact information.

  - CSS styling applied to enhance visual appeal.

Section 2: Simple Landing Page for a Product or Event

A landing page is designed to capture attention and drive visitors to take a specific action, such as signing up for an event or purchasing a product.

2.1 Explanation

A typical landing page includes:

- **A Hero Section:** Featuring a compelling headline and a call-to-action button.

- **Feature/Details Section:** Highlighting the product features or event details.

- **Sign-Up or Contact Form:** Allowing users to easily register or request more information.

2.2 Example Structure

Below is an example of a landing page structure:

```html
<!DOCTYPE html>
<html>
<head>
    <meta charset="UTF-8">
    <title>Product/Event Landing
Page</title>
    <link rel="stylesheet"
href="landing.css">
</head>
<body>
    <section class="hero">
        <h1>Introducing Our New
Product!</h1>
        <p>Discover the features and
benefits that will revolutionize your
experience.</p>
        <button id="ctaButton">Learn
More</button>
    </section>
    <section class="details">
        <h2>Why You'll Love It</h2>
        <p>Key features and advantages of
the product or event are listed here.</p>
    </section>
    <section class="signup">
        <h2>Sign Up Now</h2>
        <form id="signupForm">
            <input type="text"
placeholder="Your Name" required>
            <input type="email"
placeholder="Your Email" required>
```

```
        <button
type="submit">Submit</button>
        </form>
    </section>
</body>
</html>
```

2.3 Exercise and Action Items

- **Exercise:**

    - Create a new file named `landing.html` and build a landing page using the provided structure.

    - Integrate a call-to-action button that, when clicked, triggers an alert with a personalized message.

    - Modify the text to reflect a product or event that interests you.

- **Action Items:**

    - Use AI with a prompt like:

        "Generate CSS for a clean, modern landing page with a bold hero section and responsive form."

    - Implement the AI suggestions and then refine the layout manually.

- **Checklist:**

- A strong hero section with a headline, subheadline, and call-to-action button.

  - A detailed section that explains the product/event features.

  - A sign-up or contact form integrated into the page.

  - Responsive CSS styling applied for various screen sizes.

Section 3: Interactive Quiz Game Website

An interactive quiz game website engages users with fun, dynamic content. This project can be simple yet interactive, using JavaScript to handle quiz logic and display results.

3.1 Explanation

This project typically involves:

- **Question and Answer Interface:** Display questions with multiple choice answers.

- **Scoring Mechanism:** Track correct responses.

- **Feedback:** Provide immediate feedback and a final score at the end.

3.2 Example Structure

Below is an example of the basic structure for a quiz game:

```
<!DOCTYPE html>
```

```html
<html>
<head>
    <meta charset="UTF-8">
    <title>Interactive Quiz Game</title>
    <link rel="stylesheet" href="quiz.css">
</head>
<body>
    <h1>Quiz Time!</h1>
    <div id="quizContainer">
        <!-- Quiz questions and choices will go here -->
        <p id="question">What is the capital of France?</p>
        <button class="answer">Paris</button>
        <button class="answer">London</button>
        <button class="answer">Rome</button>
    </div>
    <p id="feedback"></p>
    <script>
        // Example JavaScript code for handling a simple quiz interaction
        const buttons = document.querySelectorAll('.answer');
        buttons.forEach(button => {
            button.addEventListener('click', function() {
                const feedback = document.getElementById('feedback');
                if (this.textContent === 'Paris') {
                    feedback.textContent = 'Correct!';
                } else {
```

```
                    feedback.textContent =
'Try again!';
                }
            });
        });
    </script>
</body>
</html>
```

3.3 Exercise and Action Items

- **Exercise:**

    - Create a file named `quiz.html` and build a simple interactive quiz page using the structure above.

    - Add at least one additional question and modify the JavaScript to handle multiple questions.

    - Test your quiz by clicking on different answers and observing the feedback.

- **Action Items:**

    - Use AI to generate a detailed quiz script by writing a prompt such as:

        "Generate JavaScript code for a quiz game that cycles through multiple questions and calculates a final score."

    - Integrate the AI-generated enhancements into your project.

- **Checklist:**

  - Display at least one quiz question with multiple answer buttons.

  - Use JavaScript to provide immediate feedback when an answer is clicked.

  - Expand the quiz to include multiple questions.

  - Ensure that the final score or feedback is displayed at the end of the quiz.

Section 4: Photo Gallery with Lightbox Effect

A photo gallery with a lightbox effect provides an engaging way to display images. When a user clicks on a thumbnail, a larger version of the image appears in a modal overlay.

4.1 Explanation

Key elements of a photo gallery with a lightbox effect include:

- **Thumbnail Gallery:** Display a grid of images.

- **Modal Window (Lightbox):** Overlay that shows the enlarged image when a thumbnail is clicked.

- **Navigation Controls:** Optional controls to browse through images in the lightbox.

4.2 Example Structure

Below is an example of a basic photo gallery with a lightbox effect:

```
<!DOCTYPE html>
<html>
<head>
    <meta charset="UTF-8">
    <title>Photo Gallery with
Lightbox</title>
    <link rel="stylesheet"
href="gallery.css">
    <style>
        /* Basic styles for the gallery and
lightbox */
        .gallery {
            display: flex;
            flex-wrap: wrap;
            gap: 10px;
        }
        .gallery img {
            width: 200px;
            cursor: pointer;
        }
        .lightbox {
            display: none;
            position: fixed;
            z-index: 10;
            top: 0;
            left: 0;
            width: 100%;
            height: 100%;
            background: rgba(0,0,0,0.8);
            justify-content: center;
            align-items: center;
        }
        .lightbox img {
```

```
                max-width: 80%;
                max-height: 80%;
            }
    </style>
</head>
<body>
    <h1>My Photo Gallery</h1>
    <div class="gallery">
        <img
src="https://via.placeholder.com/600x400"
alt="Sample Image 1" class="gallery-item">
        <img
src="https://via.placeholder.com/600x400"
alt="Sample Image 2" class="gallery-item">
        <!-- Add more images as needed -->
    </div>
    <div class="lightbox" id="lightbox">
        <img src="" alt="Expanded View"
id="lightbox-img">
    </div>
    <script>
        const galleryItems =
document.querySelectorAll('.gallery-item');
        const lightbox =
document.getElementById('lightbox');
        const lightboxImg =
document.getElementById('lightbox-img');
        galleryItems.forEach(item => {
            item.addEventListener('click',
function() {
                lightboxImg.src = this.src;
                lightbox.style.display =
'flex';
            });
        });
```

```
        lightbox.addEventListener('click',
function() {
            lightbox.style.display = 'none';
        });
    </script>
</body>
</html>
```

4.3 Exercise and Action Items

- **Exercise:**

    - Create a new file named `gallery.html` and build a photo gallery using the structure provided.

    - Replace the placeholder images with your own image URLs (or use additional placeholder images).

    - Test the lightbox effect by clicking on the thumbnails and closing the modal by clicking outside the image.

- **Action Items:**

    - Use AI to generate enhancements for the lightbox effect, such as navigation arrows. Write a prompt like:

        "Generate JavaScript and CSS for a lightbox with next and previous navigation arrows."

    - Integrate those features into your gallery project and test them.

- **Checklist:**

  - Create a grid of image thumbnails.

  - Implement a modal lightbox that displays an enlarged version of the image when clicked.

  - Allow the modal to be closed by clicking outside the image (or using a close button).

  - Test the functionality in different browsers.

Summary and Final Practice

In Chapter 10, you have worked on four mini website projects using AI to support your frontend development journey. You have learned how to:

- Build a **Personal Portfolio Page** to showcase your skills.

- Design a **Simple Landing Page** for a product or event.

- Develop an **Interactive Quiz Game Website** that engages users with dynamic content.

- Create a **Photo Gallery with a Lightbox Effect** for an enhanced image viewing experience.

Final Action Items

1. **Complete All Projects:**

- Finalize your code for each mini project (portfolio, landing page, quiz game, and photo gallery).

- Test each project in various browsers to ensure compatibility and responsiveness.

2. **Document Your Process:**

- Keep a journal of the AI prompts used, code modifications, and any issues you encountered.

- List out improvements and ideas for future enhancements.

3. **Expand and Personalize:**

- Add additional sections or custom features to each project.

- Experiment with combining two mini projects into a larger, integrated website.

Final Checklist:

- Personal Portfolio Page with header, about, projects, and contact sections.

- Landing Page with a hero section, detailed information, and a functional sign-up form.

- Interactive Quiz Game Website with multiple questions and real-time feedback.

- Photo Gallery with a responsive lightbox effect.

- All projects tested and documented.

By completing these mini projects, you've not only reinforced your understanding of HTML, CSS, and JavaScript but also learned how to leverage AI to speed up your development process and inspire creative design solutions. Continue practicing and experimenting with new ideas to build your confidence as a front-end developer.

Chapter 11: How to Expand Projects

In Chapter 11, you will learn how to take your basic website projects to the next level by expanding them into multi-page sites, making them responsive for mobile devices, and using AI to guide your next steps for upgrades. This chapter is designed to be comprehensive and beginner-friendly, providing clear explanations, real-world examples, engaging exercises, and actionable checklists to reinforce your learning.

Learning Objectives

By the end of this chapter, you will be able to:

- **Build Multi-Page Websites:**

    o Understand how to create and link multiple HTML pages.

    o Design a consistent navigation system for a multi-page site.

- **Make Websites Responsive:**

    o Learn the fundamentals of responsive design.

    o Use CSS media queries and flexible layouts to ensure your site looks good on phones and tablets.

- **Utilize AI for Site Upgrades:**

- Craft effective AI prompts to generate suggestions and code for enhancing your website.

- Identify practical "next steps" to upgrade your site's design and functionality with AI assistance.

- **Practice and Enhance Your Skills:**

  - Engage with interactive exercises and action items throughout the chapter.

  - Use checklists to track your progress and ensure you master each step.

Section 1: Adding More Pages (Multi-Page Sites)

Building a multi-page website is a natural progression from a single-page site. Multi-page sites allow you to organize content into separate sections, such as Home, About, Projects, and Contact.

1.1 Explanation: Structuring a Multi-Page Site

Multi-page websites require at least two or more HTML files. A common approach is to have a consistent header and footer on each page with unique content in between. To link these pages, you will use anchor (<a>) tags.

Example:
Imagine you are creating a personal website. You might create:

- **index.html:** Home page

- **about.html:** About section

- **projects.html:** Portfolio or projects listing

- **contact.html:** Contact form or information

1.2 Real-World Example: Basic Navigation

Here's an example of a simple navigation menu for a multi-page site:

```
<!DOCTYPE html>
<html>
<head>
    <meta charset="UTF-8">
    <title>My Personal Website -
Home</title>
    <link rel="stylesheet"
href="styles.css">
</head>
<body>
    <header>
        <nav>
            <ul>
                <li><a
href="index.html">Home</a></li>
                <li><a
href="about.html">About</a></li>
                <li><a
href="projects.html">Projects</a></li>
                <li><a
href="contact.html">Contact</a></li>
            </ul>
        </nav>
    </header>
    <main>
```

```
    <h1>Welcome to My Website!</h1>
    <p>This is the home page of my
multi-page site.</p>
  </main>
  <footer>
    <p>&copy; 2025 Your Name</p>
  </footer>
</body>
</html>
```

1.3 Exercise and Action Items

- **Exercise 1:**

  - Create four HTML files: `index.html`, `about.html`, `projects.html`, and `contact.html`.

  - Implement a navigation menu at the top of each page using the example above.

  - Customize the content of each page to reflect its purpose.

- **Action Item:**

  - Write down a plan for what content will be on each page. List the key sections for each page before coding.

Checklist for Multi-Page Sites:

- Create multiple HTML files for different sections.

- Implement consistent navigation across all pages.

- Ensure that all links work correctly in your browser.

Section 2: Making Websites Responsive for Phones

As more users access websites on mobile devices, it's important to ensure your site looks good and functions well on smaller screens.

2.1 Explanation: Basics of Responsive Design

Responsive design involves creating a flexible layout that adapts to different screen sizes. You can achieve this using:

- **CSS Media Queries:** Adjust styles based on the device's width.

- **Flexible Layouts:** Use relative units (percentages, ems, rems) instead of fixed units (pixels).

Example:
A media query adjusts the layout for screens narrower than 600px:

```
@media (max-width: 600px) {
    body {
        font-size: 16px;
        padding: 10px;
    }
    nav ul {
        flex-direction: column;
    }
    nav li {
        margin: 5px 0;
    }
```

```
}
```

2.2 Real-World Example: Responsive Navigation

Here's an example of a responsive navigation menu that switches from a horizontal layout on larger screens to a vertical layout on mobile devices:

```
<!DOCTYPE html>
<html>
<head>
    <meta charset="UTF-8">
    <title>Responsive Navigation
Example</title>
    <style>
        nav ul {
            display: flex;
            list-style: none;
            padding: 0;
        }
        nav li {
            margin: 0 15px;
        }
        @media (max-width: 600px) {
            nav ul {
                flex-direction: column;
                align-items: center;
            }
            nav li {
                margin: 10px 0;
            }
        }
    </style>
</head>
<body>
    <nav>
```

```
    <ul>
        <li><a
href="index.html">Home</a></li>
        <li><a
href="about.html">About</a></li>
        <li><a
href="projects.html">Projects</a></li>
        <li><a
href="contact.html">Contact</a></li>
    </ul>
  </nav>
  <h1>Responsive Design Example</h1>
  <p>This navigation menu adjusts based on
your screen size.</p>
</body>
</html>
```

2.3 Exercise and Action Items

- **Exercise 2:**

    - Add responsive design rules to your website's CSS.

    - Test the website on different devices or by resizing your browser window.

    - Adjust font sizes, margins, and layouts as needed for a better mobile experience.

- **Action Item:**

    - Use your browser's developer tools to simulate various device sizes and document how your site behaves on each.

Checklist for Responsive Design:

- Implement media queries in your CSS.

- Use flexible layouts and units.

- Test and adjust the design for different screen sizes.

- Verify that navigation and content remain accessible on mobile devices.

Section 3: How to Ask AI for "Next Steps" to Upgrade a Site

As you become comfortable with your current projects, you might want to enhance or upgrade your website further. AI can help you identify next steps and generate code for advanced features.

3.1 Explanation: Effective AI Prompts for Upgrades

When asking AI for advice or code to improve your site, be specific about what you want to achieve. For example:

- **Prompt Example:**

  "Generate a JavaScript code snippet that adds a smooth scrolling effect for in-page navigation links."
  "Suggest CSS enhancements to add a hover effect for navigation menu items."

Clear, detailed prompts lead to better suggestions and more usable code.

3.2 Real-World Example: AI-Guided Enhancements

Imagine you have a basic multi-page site and want to improve user experience with a dynamic feature. You might ask:

- **Prompt:**

    "Generate CSS and JavaScript code that creates a sticky navigation bar, which remains visible as the user scrolls down the page."

The AI might provide a code snippet like this:

```
/* CSS for Sticky Navigation */
header {
    position: sticky;
    top: 0;
    background: #ffffff;
    padding: 10px 0;
    box-shadow: 0 2px 5px rgba(0, 0, 0,
0.1);
}
// (Optional) Additional JavaScript if
needed for dynamic effects:
window.addEventListener('scroll', function()
{
    const header =
document.querySelector('header');
    if (window.scrollY > 50) {
        header.classList.add('scrolled');
    } else {
        header.classList.remove('scrolled');
    }
```

```
});
```

3.3 Exercise and Action Items

- **Exercise 3:**

  - Write a detailed prompt for your AI tool
    describing an upgrade feature you'd like for
    your site, such as a sticky navigation bar or
    smooth scrolling.

  - Generate the code with your AI tool.

  - Integrate the AI-generated code into one of
    your projects and test the feature.

- **Action Item:**

  - Document the prompt you used and note any
    modifications you made to the AI output.
    Analyze how these enhancements improve the
    user experience.

Checklist for Upgrading Your Site with AI:

- Write a clear prompt detailing the enhancement you
  want.

- Generate and review the AI-produced code.

- Integrate the code into your project.

- Test the new feature across different pages and
  devices.

- Document the improvements and any further tweaks needed.

Summary and Final Practice

In Chapter 11, you learned how to expand your website projects by:

- **Adding More Pages:**
  Creating multi-page sites with consistent navigation and organized content.

- **Making Websites Responsive:**
  Using CSS media queries and flexible layouts to ensure your site adapts beautifully to various devices, especially phones.

- **Utilizing AI for Upgrades:**
  Crafting effective prompts to generate upgrade suggestions and code, guiding you toward the next steps in your site's evolution.

Final Action Items

1. **Expand Your Project:**

   - Choose one of your existing projects and add at least one new page.

   - Implement a responsive design using media queries to optimize for mobile devices.

- Use AI to generate at least one advanced feature (such as a sticky navigation bar or smooth scrolling) and integrate it into your site.

2. **Document Your Process:**

   - Keep a detailed record of the AI prompts you used, the code generated, and the customizations you applied.

   - Create a checklist for future upgrades to use as a reference.

3. **Test Thoroughly:**

   - Make sure your expanded site works well on both desktop and mobile devices.

   - Check all navigation links, interactive elements, and responsive behaviors.

   - Solicit feedback from peers or mentors and make adjustments as needed.

Final Checklist:

- Expanded your website by adding multiple pages.

- Ensured all pages have a consistent navigation system.

- Implemented responsive design principles using CSS media queries.

- Successfully integrated an AI-generated enhancement.

- Tested and documented all changes.

By completing these exercises and action items, you have learned how to significantly expand and improve your website projects. With this comprehensive approach and the assistance of AI, you now have the tools and knowledge to create, enhance, and upgrade your sites confidently.

Chapter 12: Understanding and Editing AI Code

In Chapter 12, we shift our focus from generating code with AI to understanding and editing the code it produces. This chapter is essential for developing your coding skills, empowering you to read and make custom modifications to HTML, CSS, and JavaScript code. You will learn how to interpret code structures, add your personal touches, and focus on learning from examples rather than memorizing everything. With clear explanations, real-world examples, hands-on exercises, and actionable checklists, you'll grow more confident in editing and enhancing AI-generated code.

Learning Objectives

By the end of this chapter, you will be able to:

- **Read and Understand Code:**

    - Interpret the structure and purpose of HTML, CSS, and JavaScript code working together.

    - Understand how AI-generated code fits into web projects.

- **Edit and Customize AI-Generated Code:**

    - Identify parts of the code that you can modify to personalize the design or functionality.

    - Apply changes to code confidently to achieve your desired results.

- **Learn from Examples Rather Than Memorize:**

- Analyze real-world examples to see how different coding techniques are applied.

- Use these examples as a reference point for solving your coding challenges without having to memorize every detail.

- **Practice Hands-On Activities:**

  - Complete exercises that reinforce your ability to read, understand, and modify code.

  - Follow action items and checklists to track your progress and mastery of these skills.

Section 1: How to Read HTML, CSS, and JavaScript Together

Understanding how HTML, CSS, and JavaScript work together is crucial for editing AI-generated code effectively.

1.1 Explanation

- **HTML (HyperText Markup Language):**
  Provides the basic structure of the web page. Think of it as the skeleton that holds content, such as headings, paragraphs, images, and links.

- **CSS (Cascading Style Sheets):**
  Controls the presentation, including colors, fonts, layouts, and spacing. It is used to style the HTML content and make the page visually appealing.

- **JavaScript:**
  Adds interactivity and functionality to your web page. It allows you to respond to user actions (like clicks and form submissions) and update the content dynamically.

1.2 Real-World Example

Consider a simple web page with an interactive button. Below is a simplified example that combines HTML, CSS, and JavaScript:

```
<!DOCTYPE html>
<html>
<head>
    <meta charset="UTF-8">
    <title>Interactive Example</title>
    <style>
        /* CSS: Styling the page */
        body {
            font-family: Arial, sans-serif;
            background-color: #f9f9f9;
            text-align: center;
            padding: 50px;
        }
        button {
            background-color: #007BFF;
            color: #fff;
            border: none;
            padding: 15px 30px;
            font-size: 16px;
            cursor: pointer;
            border-radius: 5px;
            transition: background-color
0.3s;
        }
```

```
    button:hover {
        background-color: #0056b3;
    }
    </style>
</head>
<body>
    <!-- HTML: Structure and content -->
    <h1>Welcome to My Interactive Page</h1>
    <button id="greetButton">Click
Me!</button>
    <script>
        // JavaScript: Adding interactivity
        const greetButton =
document.getElementById('greetButton');

greetButton.addEventListener('click',
function() {
            alert('Hello, thanks for
clicking!');
        });
    </script>
</body>
</html>
```

This example shows how HTML provides the structure, CSS offers visual styling, and JavaScript adds interactivity.

1.3 Exercise and Action Items

- **Exercise:**

  - Open your text editor and create a new HTML file named `interactive-example.html`.

  - Copy the above code into your file.

- Examine the code sections for HTML, CSS, and JavaScript.

- Identify which parts of the code control the layout, the appearance, and the behavior.

- **Action Item:**

  - Write a brief summary (in your journal or notebook) describing how each code block works together.

  - Experiment by changing the button's text and background color in the CSS and observe the results.

Checklist:

- Understand the role of HTML in providing structure.

- Identify the CSS styling rules and their effects.

- Recognize the JavaScript event listener and its function.

- Document your observations and modifications.

Section 2: Adding Your Own Custom Touches

Editing AI-generated code allows you to inject your personality and creativity into your projects. Even if the code works perfectly, personal touches help make a website truly yours.

2.1 Explanation

- **Customizing Content:**
  Change text, images, and elements in the HTML to reflect your unique style or message.

- **Modifying Styles:**
  Edit the CSS to adjust colors, fonts, margins, and other visual elements. Experiment with different styles until you find the best design for your site.

- **Enhancing Functionality:**
  Tweak JavaScript functions to alter how your page responds to user interactions. This might include modifying an alert message or changing behavior on button clicks.

2.2 Real-World Example

For instance, if you have a portfolio page generated by AI, you might want to change the color scheme or add a personal introduction. Below is a modified snippet of a portfolio header:

Before (AI-generated):

```
<header>
    <h1>My Portfolio</h1>
</header>
```

After (Customized):

```
<header>
    <h1>Welcome to Jane Doe's Portfolio</h1>
    <p>Creative Designer & Front-End
Developer</p>
</header>
```

2.3 Exercise and Action Items

- **Exercise:**

  - Open one of your AI-generated projects (for example, a personal portfolio page).

  - Identify elements that you'd like to change — such as headers, paragraphs, or styles.

  - Make edits to personalize the content and visual design.

- **Action Item:**

  - Create a list of three changes you want to implement and why. Then, apply these changes and test them in your browser.

Checklist for Custom Touches:

- Modify AI-generated text to be more personal.

- Edit CSS styles (colors, fonts, layouts) to reflect your design preferences.

- Adjust JavaScript functions to customize interactions.

- Test changes and note the differences.

Section 3: Learning from Examples, Not Memorizing

The goal is to build your understanding through practical examples and experience rather than trying to memorize code. Learning to analyze and adapt code will serve you far better in the long run.

3.1 Explanation

- **Analyze and Modify:**
  Instead of copying code word-for-word, study examples and understand their structure and logic. Ask yourself how you can adapt the example to solve your specific problem.

- **Experimentation:**
  Try different variations of code to see how changes affect the output. Use AI-generated code as a starting point, and then experiment with modifications.

- **Practice Makes Perfect:**
  Regularly work on small projects or exercises that encourage you to look at code, tweak it, and see immediate results. This hands-on approach develops problem-solving skills and deepens understanding.

3.2 Real-World Example

Consider a scenario where the AI generated a piece of JavaScript for a responsive button interaction. Rather than simply using it, you might:

- Change the alert text.

- Modify the event handler to update another element on the page.

- Experiment with different event types (e.g., double-click or mouseover) to see how the behavior changes.

3.3 Exercise and Action Items

- **Exercise:**

- ○ Find an example AI-generated code snippet that you like (or use one from earlier in this chapter).

- ○ Make at least three small modifications to this code—such as changing text, color, or event types.

- ○ Test each modification and record what happens.

- **Action Item:**

  - ○ Write a brief reflection on what you learned from adjusting the code. Describe any unexpected results and how you solved them.

Checklist for Learning from Examples:

- Review AI-generated examples carefully.

- Identify parts of the code that can be modified.

- Make incremental changes and test them.

- Document what you changed and what you learned from each experiment.

Summary and Final Practice

In Chapter 12, you learned how to understand and edit AI-generated code. You now know how to:

- Read how HTML, CSS, and JavaScript work together in a web project.

- Add your personal touches to AI-generated content to make the website your own.

- Learn by examining and modifying examples rather than memorizing code.

Final Action Items

1. **Select a Project:**

   - Choose one of your AI-generated websites (such as your portfolio or landing page) and spend time reading through and understanding the entire codebase.

2. **Make Customizations:**

   - Identify at least three areas where you can add custom modifications (text changes, style tweaks, or new interactions). Make these changes and document your process.

3. **Reflect and Document:**

   - Write a summary of your experience with editing AI code. Include details on what modifications worked well, what challenges you faced, and how you solved them.

4. **Share and Get Feedback:**

   - If possible, share your modified project with peers or mentors and ask for feedback on your changes.

Final Checklist:

- Read and understand the structure of AI-generated HTML, CSS, and JavaScript.

- Make at least three custom modifications to personalize the site.

- Test the changes in your browser to confirm they work as expected.

- Document your experiments and lessons learned.

- Reflect on the process and plan further improvements based on feedback.

By engaging with these exercises and action items, you'll build the foundation for not only using AI to generate code but also taking full control by understanding, editing, and enhancing that code on your own. This skill will empower you to continually improve your websites and grow your coding expertise.

Chapter 13: Solving Problems When Things Break

In this chapter, you'll learn how to effectively troubleshoot issues that arise while developing websites. We'll cover how to ask AI for debugging help, identify common beginner mistakes, and view every error as an opportunity to improve your skills. With clear explanations, real-world examples, interactive exercises, and action items, you'll be well-equipped to diagnose and solve problems confidently.

Learning Objectives

By the end of this chapter, you will be able to:

- **Ask AI for Debugging Help:**

    o Write clear and detailed prompts when facing issues.

    o Understand how to provide context and error details for effective assistance.

- **Recognize Common Beginner Mistakes:**

    o Identify frequent errors in HTML, CSS, and JavaScript.

    o Apply best practices to avoid or fix these mistakes.

- **Embrace Errors as Learning Opportunities:**

    o Analyze errors to learn and improve your coding skills.

- Use systematic debugging techniques to resolve issues and grow as a developer.

- **Practice and Reinforce Debugging Skills:**

  - Engage with exercises and use checklists to track your troubleshooting process.

  - Apply new strategies to real-world scenarios to build your confidence in resolving coding problems.

Section 1: How to Ask AI for Debugging Help

When something isn't working, knowing how to ask for help is a crucial skill. AI can be a powerful partner in debugging if you provide clear, detailed information.

Explanation

When seeking debugging help from AI:

- **Be Specific:**
  Describe the problem clearly. Include the exact error messages, the environment (browser, version, etc.), and the line(s) of code where the issue occurs.

- **Share Your Code:**
  Provide the relevant code snippet that is causing the error. More context results in better help.

- **Explain What You Expected:**
  Mention what you intended to happen versus what is actually happening. This contrast can help pinpoint the problem.

Real-World Example

Imagine you are developing a button that should display an alert when clicked, but nothing happens. Instead of saying, "My button doesn't work," a good prompt might be:

> "I have a button with the ID 'alertButton' that should trigger an alert. When I click it in Chrome, nothing happens, and no errors appear in the console. Here's my code snippet:

```
<button id="alertButton">Click Me!</button>
<script>

document.getElementById('alertButton').addEv
entListener('click', function() {
        alert('Button clicked!');
    });
</script>
```

> What might be wrong with my code or setup?"

This prompt provides context, code, and your expectation, making it easier for the AI (or another helper) to diagnose the issue.

Exercise 1: Craft Your Debugging Prompt

- **Task:**
  Create a prompt for AI to help debug a scenario where a form's submit button isn't working as expected.

- **Steps:**

    1. Write down the error message (or note that no message appears).

2. Include a brief description of your expected behavior.

3. Provide a short code snippet of your form and JavaScript handling its submission.

- **Action Item:**
  Compare your prompt with a partner or mentor and refine it to be as clear and detailed as possible.

Checklist for Effective Debugging Prompts:

- Clearly state the problem and expected outcome.

- Include relevant code snippets.

- Describe the environment (browser, OS, etc.) if applicable.

- Ask a specific question for targeted help.

Section 2: Common Beginner Mistakes

Every developer makes mistakes, especially when you're just starting. Knowing what common errors to watch out for can save you a lot of time and frustration.

Explanation

Some of the most frequent beginner mistakes include:

- **Unclosed HTML Tags:**
  Leaving out closing tags (for example, not closing `<p>` or `<div>`) can break the structure of your page.

- **Typos in CSS or JavaScript:**
  Misspelling property names (e.g., writing `colr` instead of `color`) or variable names can stop your code from working properly.

- **Incorrect Use of Syntax:**
  Missing semicolons in JavaScript, extra commas, or misplacement of braces can cause errors.

- **Wrong File Paths:**
  Linking to external stylesheets or scripts with incorrect file paths prevents your code from loading.

Real-World Examples
HTML Example:

```
<!-- Mistake: Missing closing tag for <p> -->
<p>This paragraph is not closed properly.
```

CSS Example:

```
/* Mistake: Misspelled property 'colr' */
h1 {
    colr: #333;
}
```

JavaScript Example:

```
// Mistake: Missing semicolon
const greeting = 'Hello'
console.log(greeting)
```

Exercise 2: Identify and Fix Errors

Task:

Review the following code snippet and identify three common mistakes:

```html
<html>
  <head>
    <title>Test Page<title>
    <link rel="stylesheet"
href="styles.css">
  </head>
  <body>
    <h1>Welcome to the Test Page</h1>
    <p>This is a test page.
    <button id="testBtn">Click Me</button>
    <script>
        const testBtn =
document.getElementById('testBtn')
        testBtn.addEventListener('click',
function() {
            console.log('Button was
clicked')
        )
    </script>
  </body>
</html>
```

- **Action Item:**
  Identify and correct the mistakes in the code. Then, run the corrected code in your browser to see if it behaves as expected.

Checklist for Common Mistakes:

- Ensure all HTML tags are correctly opened and closed.

160

- Check for spelling errors in CSS properties and JavaScript variables.

- Verify proper usage of semicolons, braces, and punctuation.

- Confirm that file paths in `<link>` and `<script>` tags are correct.

Section 3: Why Every Error Is a Learning Opportunity

Errors can be frustrating, but each one is a chance to learn something new. Embracing errors helps you develop robust debugging and problem-solving skills.

Explanation

- **Analyze the Error:**
  Take time to read error messages carefully. They often provide clues about what went wrong and where to look.

- **Experiment and Learn:**
  Try different solutions, compare your results, and see what works. This experimentation will expand your understanding of coding.

- **Document Your Lessons:**
  Keep a log or journal of errors and what you learned from them. Over time, you'll develop a personal troubleshooting guide.

Real-World Example

Suppose you made a mistake by forgetting to close an HTML tag, and the page layout broke. After fixing the error, you learn the importance of validating your code. You might then use an HTML validator tool regularly as part of your development process.

Exercise 3: Reflect on an Error

- **Task:**
  Think of a recent error you encountered (or use a sample error from this chapter). Write a brief reflection addressing:

  - What caused the error.

  - How you identified and fixed it.

  - What you learned that will help prevent similar issues in the future.

- **Action Item:**
  Share your reflection with a peer or mentor to discuss alternative debugging approaches.

Checklist for Viewing Errors as Learning Opportunities:

- Analyze error messages thoroughly.

- Experiment with different fixes and document outcomes.

- Maintain a log of errors and solutions.

- Reflect on each error to build deeper understanding and prevent recurrence.

Summary and Final Practice

In Chapter 13, you learned how to solve problems when things break by mastering debugging techniques. You now know how to:

- **Ask AI for Debugging Help:**
  Formulate clear, detailed prompts to help diagnose and resolve issues.

- **Identify Common Beginner Mistakes:**
  Recognize frequent errors in HTML, CSS, and JavaScript and apply strategies to fix them.

- **Embrace Errors as Learning Opportunities:**
  Use each error as a chance to learn, experiment, and improve your coding skills.

Final Action Items

1. **Practice Debugging:**

   - Choose one of your recent projects that had errors.

   - Write a detailed AI prompt asking for debugging help, incorporating specifics such as error messages and expected behavior.

   - Apply the AI suggestions, fix the errors, and document the changes you made.

2. **Reflect on a Recent Error:**

- Write a short journal entry describing a challenge you encountered, what you learned, and how you would handle it differently next time.

3. **Create a Personal Troubleshooting Checklist:**

   - Compile a list of common errors you've encountered.

   - Include steps for verifying and debugging each type of error.

   - Review this checklist each time you face a new issue.

Final Checklist:

- Formulate and test an AI debugging prompt.

- Identify and fix at least three common mistakes in a sample code snippet.

- Reflect on an error and document your learning.

- Create and use a personal troubleshooting checklist for future projects.

By engaging with the exercises and action items in this chapter, you'll build robust debugging skills and a positive mindset toward problem-solving. Remember, every error is an opportunity to learn and grow as a developer.

Chapter 14: Your Next Steps

In this final chapter, we explore the next steps in your journey to becoming a confident front-end developer with the help of AI. In this chapter, you will learn how to host your website using simple and free methods, explore advanced topics like animations, APIs, and frameworks such as Bootstrap, and discover ways to become even more creative with your websites. This chapter provides clear explanations, practical examples, exercises, and action items to help you take your skills further.

Learning Objectives

By the end of this chapter, you will be able to:

- **Host Your Website:**

    - Understand what website hosting is and why it's important.

    - Learn simple, free hosting methods (such as GitHub Pages or Netlify) to publish your site online.

- **Explore Advanced Topics:**

    - Implement basic animations using CSS or JavaScript.

    - Integrate external data with APIs into your website.

    - Utilize Bootstrap (or other frameworks) to create responsive, polished designs.

- **Become More Creative with Your Websites:**

  - Experiment with new design ideas and interactive elements.

  - Use creative AI prompts to generate unique features and enhancements.

  - Develop a mindset of continuous improvement and exploration.

- **Practice and Reinforce New Skills:**

  - Engage in exercises that apply hosting, advanced design techniques, and creative enhancements.

  - Use checklists and action items to track your progress as you experiment and build on your projects.

Section 1: Learning About Hosting Your Website

Hosting is the process of making your website accessible on the internet so that others can view it. For beginners, there are many free and simple ways to host your website.

1.1 Explanation: What Is Hosting and Why It Matters

- **Definition:**
  Hosting means storing your website's files on a server that is connected to the internet. When someone visits your URL, the server sends the website files to their browser.

- **Why It Matters:**
  Hosting makes your website available to a global audience. It also often provides additional features like security, domain management, and scalability.

1.2 Free and Simple Hosting Options

- **GitHub Pages:**
  Allows you to host static websites (HTML, CSS, and JavaScript) directly from your GitHub repository. It is free and relatively simple if you have a GitHub account.

- **Netlify:**
  Offers free hosting along with continuous deployment, meaning your site can automatically update whenever you push changes to your repository.

- **Other Options:**
  Other services like Vercel, Firebase Hosting, or even WordPress.com for static content offer free tiers that are beginner-friendly.

1.3 Real-World Example: Hosting with GitHub Pages

Step-by-Step Overview:

1. **Create a Repository:**
   On GitHub, create a new repository (e.g., "my-first-website").

2. **Upload Your Website Files:**
   Add your `index.html`, `styles.css`, and any other assets.

3. **Enable GitHub Pages:**
   Go to the repository settings and enable GitHub Pages, selecting the branch (usually `main` or `master`).

4. **Access Your Website:**
   GitHub provides a URL (e.g., `https://username.github.io/my-first-website/`) where your site is hosted.

Exercise 1: Host Your Website

- **Task:**
  Host one of your completed projects (for example, your personal portfolio page) on GitHub Pages.

- **Steps:**

  1. Create a new repository on GitHub.

  2. Push your project files to that repository.

  3. Follow the instructions in the repository settings to enable GitHub Pages.

  4. Visit the provided URL to see your live website.

- **Action Item:**
  Document the steps you followed and note any challenges you encountered. Try making a small update and see if the site updates automatically when you push the changes.

Checklist:

- Create a GitHub repository for your project.

- Upload or push all website files.

- Enable GitHub Pages in repository settings.

- Confirm that your website is accessible via the provided URL.

Section 2: Exploring Advanced Topics

Once you are comfortable with basic website creation and hosting, you can start exploring more advanced topics. This section introduces you to animations, APIs, and frameworks like Bootstrap to enhance your site.

2.1 Implementing Animations

Animations can make your website more engaging by drawing attention to elements or guiding users through interactions.

Explanation

- **CSS Animations:**
  Use keyframes and transitions to animate properties like color, position, and opacity.

- **JavaScript Animations:**
  For more dynamic or complex animations, JavaScript can manipulate element properties over time.

Real-World Example: Simple Button Hover Animation

```
button {
    background-color: #007BFF;
    color: white;
```

```
    border: none;
    padding: 12px 24px;
    transition: transform 0.3s ease;
}
button:hover {
    transform: scale(1.1);
}
```

Exercise 2: Add an Animation

- **Task:**
  Modify one of your existing projects by adding a hover animation to a button or image.

- **Steps:**

    1. Choose an element to animate (e.g., a button).

    2. Write CSS rules with transitions and hover effects.

    3. Test the animation in your browser.

- **Action Item:**
  Experiment with different timing values (e.g., transition duration) and document how the changes affect the animation.

Checklist:

- Select an element to animate.

- Add CSS transitions and keyframes if needed.

- Test and observe the animation on hover.

- Adjust values for desired effect.

2.2 Integrating APIs

APIs (Application Programming Interfaces) allow your website to communicate with external services and retrieve data. For example, you might use an API to display the current weather or fetch news headlines.

Explanation

- **How APIs Work:**
  APIs provide endpoints (URLs) that return data in formats like JSON. JavaScript can call these endpoints using functions such as `fetch()`.

Real-World Example: Fetching Data from a Public API

```
fetch('https://api.example.com/data')
    .then(response => response.json())
    .then(data => {
        console.log('Data from API:', data);
        // Update your webpage with the
received data
    })
    .catch(error => console.error('Error
fetching data:', error));
```

Exercise 3: Use an API

- **Task:**
  Use a public API (for example, a weather API or a joke API) to retrieve data and display it on your website.

- **Steps:**

1. Choose a simple public API.

2. Write JavaScript to call the API and display the data on your page.

3. Style the output as needed.

- **Action Item:**
  Document your process, including the API endpoint you used, your code, and how the data is integrated into your site.

Checklist:

- Choose a reliable public API.

- Write JavaScript code using the `fetch()` method.

- Parse the API response and display it.

- Handle errors gracefully.

2.3 Utilizing Bootstrap for Responsive Design

Bootstrap is a popular CSS framework that helps you quickly create responsive and modern websites.

Explanation

- **Bootstrap Features:**
  Provides pre-designed components such as grids, buttons, and navigation elements.

- **How to Use:**
  Include Bootstrap's CSS and JavaScript files (via a CDN or locally) in your HTML, then apply its classes to your elements.

Real-World Example: Simple Bootstrap Grid

```
<!DOCTYPE html>
<html>
<head>
    <meta charset="UTF-8">
    <title>Bootstrap Example</title>
    <!-- Include Bootstrap CSS -->
    <link rel="stylesheet"
href="https://stackpath.bootstrapcdn.com/boo
tstrap/4.5.2/css/bootstrap.min.css">
</head>
<body>
    <div class="container">
        <div class="row">
            <div class="col-md-4">
                <h2>Column 1</h2>
                <p>Content for the first
column.</p>
            </div>
            <div class="col-md-4">
                <h2>Column 2</h2>
                <p>Content for the second
column.</p>
            </div>
            <div class="col-md-4">
                <h2>Column 3</h2>
                <p>Content for the third
column.</p>
            </div>
        </div>
```

```
    </div>
    <!-- Include Bootstrap JS (optional) -->
    <script
src="https://code.jquery.com/jquery-
3.5.1.slim.min.js"></script>
    <script
src="https://stackpath.bootstrapcdn.com/boot
strap/4.5.2/js/bootstrap.min.js"></script>
</body>
</html>
```

Exercise 4: Apply Bootstrap to a Project

- **Task:**
  Select one of your existing projects and integrate
  Bootstrap to improve its layout and responsiveness.

- **Steps:**

  1. Include Bootstrap via CDN in your HTML file.

  2. Replace or augment your current layout with
     Bootstrap grid classes.

  3. Test the result in your browser and adjust as
     necessary.

- **Action Item:**
  Experiment with different Bootstrap components
  (e.g., navbars or cards) and note how they enhance
  the design.

Checklist:

- Include Bootstrap's CSS and JS files in your project.

- Apply Bootstrap classes to create a responsive grid layout.

- Test and refine the design for various screen sizes.

- Document the changes and improvements.

Section 3: Becoming More Creative with Your Websites

As you gain more technical skills, it's time to let your creativity shine. Your websites can reflect your personality, style, and ideas. AI can help inspire creative features and designs, but the real magic happens when you customize and innovate.

3.1 Explanation: Exploring Creative Possibilities

- **Design Inspiration:**
  Use AI prompts to generate creative ideas or design suggestions. For example, ask for trendy color schemes, dynamic animations, or unique layout structures.

- **Custom Features:**
  Combine AI-generated code with your own ideas. Don't be afraid to experiment by adding custom effects, interactive elements, or personalized content.

- **Iterative Improvement:**
  Creativity often requires experimentation. Tweak, test, and refine your websites based on feedback and personal insight.

3.2 Real-World Example: A Creative Homepage

Imagine a homepage that uses a background video, creative typography, and interactive animations. AI might provide a starting point for the animation or layout, which you then customize by changing styles, texts, and effects to reflect your vision.

Sample Prompt for AI:

> "Generate CSS that creates an animated gradient background for a homepage header with smooth transitions between colors."

Exercise 5: Unleash Your Creativity

- **Task:**
  Choose one project and add a creative feature that isn't strictly required by functionality. This could be a custom animated background, an interactive infographic, or a unique navigation effect.

- **Steps:**

  1. Write a prompt for your AI tool that describes your creative feature.

  2. Integrate the generated code into your project.

  3. Refine the code to match your personal style and vision.

- **Action Item:**
  Reflect on the creative process by writing down the inspiration behind your feature and the specific modifications you made.

Checklist for Creative Websites:

- Use AI prompts to generate design ideas.

- Integrate a creative feature into your project.

- Customize the feature to reflect your personal style.

- Test and refine the interactive or visual elements.

Summary and Final Action Items

In Chapter 14, you explored the next steps you can take to enhance your web development skills. You learned how to:

- **Host Your Website:**
  Use simple and free hosting solutions such as GitHub Pages or Netlify to make your site publicly available.

- **Explore Advanced Topics:**
  Dive into animations, API integrations, and responsive design using tools like CSS, JavaScript, and Bootstrap.

- **Become More Creative:**
  Combine AI-generated suggestions with your personal ideas to create unique, dynamic, and engaging websites.

Final Action Items

1. **Host a Project:**

   o Choose one of your projects and host it using one of the free hosting services.

○ Test your live site and share the URL with peers for feedback.

2. **Implement an Advanced Feature:**

   ○ Add at least one advanced feature (e.g., animations, API integration, or a Bootstrap layout) to an existing project.

   ○ Document the process and the benefits the feature brings to the user experience.

3. **Enhance Your Creative Side:**

   ○ Brainstorm a creative idea for your website.

   ○ Use AI prompts to generate a starting point.

   ○ Customize and refine the feature until it truly reflects your style.

4. **Document Your Journey:**

   ○ Keep a journal of your experiences, noting which techniques worked well, what challenges arose, and how you solved them.

   ○ Develop a personal checklist for future projects that outlines your steps from design to deployment.

Final Checklist:

- Host your website on a free platform.

- Implement an advanced feature using animations, APIs, or Bootstrap.

- Enhance your project with a creative, personalized touch.

- Thoroughly test your website on various devices and browsers.

- Document each step and reflect on your progress.

By following these steps and engaging with the exercises, you're setting yourself up for continued success as a front-end developer. Remember, every new project is an opportunity to learn, experiment, and grow your skills further.

Bonus Section: Cheat Sheets for Non-Coders

This bonus section is designed to serve as a quick-reference guide for all the essential elements of front-end web development. Whether you're a beginner or need a refresher, these cheat sheets will help you navigate your coding journey with ease. In this section, we provide:

- A list of the top 10 HTML tags you'll use repeatedly.

- The top 10 CSS properties that can transform your designs.

- Example JavaScript tricks for interactive features.

- Ready-to-use prompts to copy, customize, and boost your productivity.

- A quick troubleshooting guide to help you fix common problems.

- Final thoughts to inspire your continued learning and creativity.

Learning Objectives

By the end of this bonus section, you will be able to:

- **Recall Essential HTML Tags:**
  Understand and quickly reference the most commonly used HTML tags and their purposes.

- **Utilize Key CSS Properties:**
  Know which CSS properties will most often enhance your website's appearance and how to use them.

- **Implement Simple JavaScript Tricks:**
  Learn a few simple JavaScript tricks to add interactivity to your pages without getting overwhelmed.

- **Leverage Customizable AI Prompts:**
  Use example prompts to generate code and design ideas, then customize them to fit your project needs.

- **Troubleshoot Common Issues:**
  Follow a quick troubleshooting guide for resolving frequent errors and problems in your code.

- **Incorporate These Tools as Part of Your Workflow:**
  Use these cheat sheets to build your projects faster and with confidence.

Section 1: Top 10 HTML Tags You'll Use All the Time

HTML is the backbone of your website. Here are ten essential tags every non-coder should be familiar with:

1. **`<html>`**

    - **Purpose:** Wraps all the content on your web page.

Example:

```
<html> ... </html>
```

2. **\<head\>**

   - **Purpose:** Contains meta-information, like the title and links to stylesheets.

Example:

```
<head>
    <title>My Page Title</title>
</head>
```

3. **\<body\>**

   - **Purpose:** Contains all the content visible on the webpage.

Example:

```
<body>
    <p>Welcome to my website!</p>
</body>
```

4. **\<h1\> to \<h6\>**

   - **Purpose:** Create headings; \<h1\> is the most important, \<h6\> is the least.

Example:

```
<h1>Main Heading</h1>
<h2>Subheading</h2>
```

5. **\<p\>**

○ **Purpose:** Defines a paragraph.

Example:

```
<p>This is a paragraph of text.</p>
```

6. **<a>**

    ○ **Purpose:** Creates hyperlinks.

Example:

```
<a href="https://www.example.com">Visit
Example.com</a>
```

7. **<img>**

    ○ **Purpose:** Embeds images.

Example:

```
<img src="image-url.jpg" alt="Description of
image">
```

8. **<ul>, <ol>, <li>**

    ○ **Purpose:** Create unordered (bullet points) and
      ordered (numbered) lists.

Example:

```
<ul>
    <li>Item 1</li>
    <li>Item 2</li>
</ul>
```

9. **`<div>`**

   o **Purpose:** A container that groups other HTML elements.

Example:

```
<div class="container">
    <p>Content inside a division.</p>
</div>
```

10. **`<span>`**

    o **Purpose:** Applies styles or interactions to a small chunk of text inline.

Example:

```
<p>This is <span style="color:
red;">important</span> text.</p>
```

Exercise:
Create a simple webpage that uses each of these tags at least once. Write a brief description next to each example in your code comments explaining its purpose.

Action Items:

- Experiment with each tag by creating a sample HTML file.

- Use a checklist (see below) to ensure you include all essential tags.

Checklist:

- `<html>`

- `<head>`

- `<body>`

- Heading tags (`<h1>` to `<h6>`)

- `<p>`

- `<a>`

- `<img>`

- List tags (`<ul>`, `<ol>`, `<li>`)

- `<div>`

- `<span>`

Section 2: Top 10 CSS Properties You'll Love

CSS properties are the tools you use to style your website. Here are ten important properties that enhance your design:

1. **color**

   ○ **Purpose:** Sets the color of text.

Example:

```
p {
    color: #333333;
}
```

2. **background-color**

   ○ **Purpose:** Sets the background color of an element.

Example:

```
body {
    background-color: #f0f0f0;
}
```

3. **font-family**

   ○ **Purpose:** Determines the typeface for text.

Example:

```
body {
    font-family: Arial, sans-serif;
}
```

4. **font-size**

   ○ **Purpose:** Sets the size of the text.

Example:

```
h1 {
    font-size: 2em;
}
```

5. **margin**

- **Purpose:** Creates space outside of elements.

Example:

```css
.container {
    margin: 20px;
}
```

6. **padding**

- **Purpose:** Creates space inside of elements.

Example:

```css
.container {
    padding: 20px;
}
```

7. **border**

- **Purpose:** Adds a border around elements.

Example:

```css
img {
    border: 2px solid #000;
}
```

8. **display**

- **Purpose:** Controls how an element is displayed (block, inline, etc.).

Example:

```
div {
    display: block;
}
```

9. **flex**

- ○ **Purpose:** Used with flexbox layouts to easily arrange elements.

Example:

```
.flex-container {
    display: flex;
    justify-content: center;
    align-items: center;
}
```

10. **transition**

- ○ **Purpose:** Creates smooth animations between state changes.

Example:

```
button {
    transition: background-color 0.3s ease;
}
button:hover {
    background-color: #555;
}
```

Exercise:

Create a stylesheet (`styles.css`) that applies each of these properties to different elements on your test webpage. Experiment with different values to see their visual effects.

Action Items:

- Save your stylesheet and link it to an HTML file.

- Use the checklist below to ensure every property is implemented at least once.

Checklist:

- `color`

- `background-color`

- `font-family`

- `font-size`

- `margin`

- `padding`

- `border`

- `display`

- `flex`

- `transition`

Section 3: Example JavaScript Tricks for Beginners

JavaScript can add a great deal of interactivity to your websites. Here are some simple tricks that can help you make your pages dynamic:

Alert on Button Click:

```
document.getElementById('myButton').addEvent
Listener('click', function() {
    alert('Button clicked!');
});
```
Change Text on Hover:

```
document.getElementById('hoverText').addEven
tListener('mouseover', function() {
    this.textContent = 'You hovered over
me!';
});
```
Toggle a Class:

```
document.getElementById('toggleButton').addE
ventListener('click', function() {

document.getElementById('myElement').classLi
st.toggle('active');
});
```
Simple Form Validation:

```
document.getElementById('submitForm').addEve
ntListener('submit', function(e) {
    e.preventDefault();
    const nameInput =
document.getElementById('nameInput').value;
    if (nameInput.trim() === '') {
```

```
        alert('Please enter your name.');
    } else {
        alert('Form submitted!');
    }
});
```

1. **Image Slideshow:**
   Basic idea: Cycle through a set of images by changing the src attribute of an image element.
   (Write your own version or ask AI for a detailed example.)

Exercise:

Create a simple JavaScript file (script.js) that includes at least two of these tricks. Link it to an HTML page and test each functionality.

Action Items:

- Experiment by modifying the examples (e.g., change alert messages, text replacements, etc.).

- Document your changes and observe how the interactivity improves the user experience.

Checklist:

- Implement an alert on button click.

- Add a hover effect that changes text.

- Try toggling a class on an element.

- Incorporate basic form validation.

- Experiment with additional JavaScript interactions.

Section 4: Example Prompts to Copy and Customize

Here are several AI prompt examples that you can copy, tweak, and use for your projects:

1. **HTML Prompt:**

   "Generate HTML code for a simple personal bio section with a header, a profile picture, a short description, and a link to my portfolio."

2. **CSS Prompt:**

   "Generate CSS for a modern and minimalist website with a clean layout, soft colors, and responsive design using a flexbox layout."

3. **JavaScript Prompt:**

   "Generate JavaScript code for a form that validates user input for name and email, displaying a custom alert if fields are empty."

4. **Combined Prompt:**

   "Generate a multi-page website template with a header, footer, and a navigation menu. Include CSS for styling and JavaScript for smooth scrolling between pages."

5. **Debugging Prompt:**

   "I have an issue where my button click event isn't working. Here's my code snippet. Please help me identify the error and provide a fix."

Exercise:
Copy one of these prompts and try it in your AI tool. Customize the generated code, then integrate it into one of your projects.

Action Items:

- Keep a log of prompts you use.

- Note any modifications you make and record the outcomes.

- Experiment with different variations to see which results work best for your project.

Section 5: Quick Troubleshooting Guide

When errors occur, keep this quick guide handy:

- **Check Your Console:**
  Open your browser's developer tools (usually F12 or right-click and "Inspect") to see error messages.

- **Validate Your HTML/CSS:**
  Use online validators to check for missing tags or syntax errors.

- **Review File Paths:**
  Ensure that all file paths for images, stylesheets, and scripts are correct.

- **Isolate the Problem:**
  Comment out sections of code to isolate what might be causing the error.

- **Ask for Help:**
  Use clear, detailed prompts when asking AI or peers for debugging assistance.

- **Take Breaks:**
  Sometimes a short break can help you see the problem in a new light.

Checklist for Troubleshooting:

- Open the browser console to review errors.

- Validate code for HTML and CSS errors.

- Confirm all file paths are correct.

- Isolate problematic code segments.

- Formulate a clear prompt for debugging help if needed.

Section 6: Final Thoughts

This bonus section has provided you with handy cheat sheets and practical examples to use throughout your front-end development journey. Remember:

- **Cheat Sheets Are Tools:**
  They are meant to be reference points to make your work easier, not crutches to hold you back.

- **Practice Regularly:**
  The more you experiment with these tags, properties, JavaScript tricks, and prompts, the more confident you will become.

- **Learn from Every Project:**
  Every error, every modification, and every successful feature builds your skill set. Don't be afraid to make mistakes — they are integral to learning.

- **Stay Creative:**
  Use AI as a partner to spark ideas, but always add your own creative twist to make your projects truly unique.

Final Action Items:

1. **Review and Bookmark:**

   - Save this section as a reference document on your computer.

   - Review it when working on new projects or when you face challenges.

2. **Apply Regularly:**

   o Use the cheat sheets to guide your coding sessions.

   o Experiment with the prompts and troubleshooting tips.

3. **Reflect and Document:**

   o Maintain a coding journal where you record what you've learned.

   o Update your cheat sheets as you discover new tools, prompts, or techniques.

Final Checklist:

- Memorize (or bookmark) the top 10 HTML tags.

- Know the top 10 CSS properties and practice using them.

- Try at least two JavaScript tricks on your projects.

- Use provided example prompts and refine them to suit your needs.

- Keep the troubleshooting guide handy for when issues arise.

- Document your learning journey and reflect on your progress.

By integrating these cheat sheets into your workflow, you'll have a fast, accessible reference to support you as you continue to build amazing websites using AI. Let these resources help streamline your projects and empower you to be innovative, efficient, and creative in your coding adventures.

Test Your Knowledge

Chapter 1: What is Front-End Development? (7 Questions)

Question 1.1:
Which of the following technologies is primarily used to define the structure and content of a webpage?
A) CSS
B) HTML
C) JavaScript
D) PHP

Answer: B – HTML
Explanation: HTML (HyperText Markup Language) is the standard markup language used to create the structure of web pages. It provides the basic skeleton for content such as headings, paragraphs, images, and links.

Question 1.2:
What is the main purpose of CSS in web development?
A) To create dynamic interactions
B) To handle server-side logic
C) To style and visually arrange webpage elements
D) To manage website databases

Answer: C – To style and visually arrange webpage elements
Explanation: CSS (Cascading Style Sheets) is used to control the presentation of HTML elements — such as colors, layouts, fonts, and spacing — making websites visually appealing.

Question 1.3:

Which language is used primarily to add interactivity to web pages?

A) HTML
B) CSS
C) JavaScript
D) SQL

Answer: C – JavaScript

Explanation: JavaScript allows developers to add dynamic behavior and interactivity (such as responding to button clicks, updating content, or validating forms) to web pages.

Question 1.4:

In a typical front-end development project, what role does HTML play?

A) It serves as a programming language for interactivity.
B) It provides the structure and layout for content.
C) It styles and visually transforms content.
D) It manages server-side operations.

Answer: B – It provides the structure and layout for content.

Explanation: HTML is the foundation of a web page that defines its structure. It organizes content into headings, paragraphs, images, links, etc.

Question 1.5:

Which combination of technologies is considered essential for front-end development?

A) HTML, CSS, JavaScript
B) HTML, PHP, SQL
C) CSS, Python, Ruby
D) JavaScript, C++, Java

Answer: A – HTML, CSS, JavaScript

Explanation: HTML, CSS, and JavaScript form the core trio for front-end development: HTML structures, CSS styles, and JavaScript adds interactivity.

Question 1.6:
Why is front-end development important for creating websites?
A) It manages database connections.
B) It controls user interface elements that visitors interact with.
C) It handles network and server security exclusively.
D) It processes back-end business logic.

Answer: B – It controls user interface elements that visitors interact with.
Explanation: Front-end development focuses on the visual aspects and user interactions, making the website accessible and user-friendly.

Question 1.7:
Which technology would you use to structure a webpage's content into sections, headings, and paragraphs?
A) JavaScript
B) HTML
C) CSS
D) JSON

Answer: B – HTML
Explanation: HTML provides the semantic elements used to create well-structured content (e.g., `<header>`, `<section>`, `<p>`, etc.) on a webpage.

Chapter 2: Setting Up Your Playground (7 Questions)

Question 2.1:
What is one major advantage of using an online code editor such as CodePen or JSFiddle for beginners?
A) It requires manual installation of software.
B) It provides instant preview without local setup.
C) It only supports advanced coding languages.
D) It restricts collaboration with others.

Answer: B – It provides instant preview without local setup.
Explanation: Online editors allow you to write, test, and view your code immediately in a browser, simplifying the process for beginners without needing any installations.

Question 2.2:
Which online editor is known for its ability to let you create and share "pens" with live previews?
A) Eclipse
B) CodePen
C) Vim
D) Sublime Text

Answer: B – CodePen
Explanation: CodePen is a popular online editor designed for front-end development that lets you create "pens" with HTML, CSS, and JavaScript, showing a live preview as you code.

Question 2.3:
When setting up your playground, what is the primary purpose of having a live preview feature?
A) To see real-time syntax errors without running the code
B) To compile code into machine language
C) To instantly visualize the output of your code as you write it
D) To edit backend code

Answer: C – To instantly visualize the output of your code as you write it
Explanation: The live preview provides immediate feedback on how your code affects the webpage, allowing you to learn and iterate quickly.

Question 2.4:
Which of the following is an optional tool mentioned for those who want to eventually move to a full-featured code editor?
A) GitHub Pages
B) Visual Studio Code
C) Netlify
D) Heroku

Answer: B – Visual Studio Code
Explanation: Visual Studio Code (VS Code) is a powerful and customizable code editor that many developers use once they're comfortable with the basics from online editors.

Question 2.5:
What benefit does an online code editor offer for collaboration?
A) It prevents code sharing.
B) It requires complex installation for each user.
C) It allows users to share live links to their projects easily.
D) It only works on a local machine.

Answer: C – It allows users to share live links to their projects easily.
Explanation: Online editors make collaboration simple by providing URLs that can be shared with others for real-time viewing and feedback.

Question 2.6:
Which feature is common in online editors like Replit that supports not only front-end but also multi-language development?
A) Built-in video tutorials
B) Integrated server-side and client-side coding environments
C) Automatic translation of code
D) Hardware-based debugging

Answer: B – Integrated server-side and client-side coding environments
Explanation: Replit supports many programming languages and offers an integrated environment that can be used for both front-end and back-end development, making it versatile for learning.

Question 2.7:
Why might a beginner choose an online editor over installing software like Visual Studio Code?
A) Online editors are less flexible.
B) They require no installation and provide instant feedback.
C) They only support outdated languages.
D) They offer fewer learning resources.

Answer: B – They require no installation and provide instant feedback.
Explanation: Online editors are ideal for beginners because they eliminate the need for local setup, making the initial learning process smoother and more accessible.

Chapter 3: Meeting Your AI Website Builder Assistant (7 Questions)

Question 3.1:
What is one major benefit of using AI tools in web development for non-coders?
A) AI replaces the need to learn any coding principles.
B) AI helps generate code snippets and design ideas quickly.
C) AI makes testing your website unnecessary.
D) AI primarily handles server maintenance.

Answer: B – AI helps generate code snippets and design ideas quickly.

Explanation: AI tools can provide helpful code examples and creative suggestions that accelerate the development process, making coding more accessible for non-coders.

Question 3.2:

When asking AI for website code, which of the following is most important?
A) Using very general requests
B) Providing clear, detailed prompts
C) Asking for code without context
D) Avoiding any descriptions of design needs

Answer: B – Providing clear, detailed prompts

Explanation: Detailed prompts help the AI understand exactly what you need, leading to more useful and relevant code output.

Question 3.3:

What should you include in your prompt if you want AI to generate a navigation bar?
A) Only the word "navigation"
B) Specific design requirements like "responsive," "horizontal layout," and "dropdown menu"
C) A random string of characters
D) No details at all

Answer: B – Specific design requirements like "responsive," "horizontal layout," and "dropdown menu"

Explanation: Detailed prompts that list design requirements provide the AI with enough context to generate code that meets your expectations.

Question 3.4:
How can AI help non-coders become more confident in web development?
A) By completely automating the development process
B) By generating error-free, perfectly customized code without any human input
C) By acting as a guide that teaches through code examples and suggestions
D) By restricting the available design options

Answer: C – By acting as a guide that teaches through code examples and suggestions
Explanation: AI tools offer practical code examples and tailored suggestions that help beginners learn coding practices and build confidence gradually.

Question 3.5:
What is a key limitation of relying solely on AI for website development?
A) AI cannot generate any HTML code
B) AI might produce generic code that still requires customization
C) AI always produces perfect and creative designs
D) AI eliminates the need for debugging

Answer: B – AI might produce generic code that still requires customization
Explanation: While AI is a useful assistant, it may generate code that is not fully tailored to your unique needs. It's essential to review, understand, and modify the code accordingly.

Question 3.6:
When an AI assistant gives you code suggestions, what should you do next?
A) Blindly copy the code without testing
B) Review the code to understand how it works and tailor it to your project
C) Delete the code and start from scratch
D) Only use the code for non-functional prototypes

Answer: B – Review the code to understand how it works and tailor it to your project
Explanation: It is important to read and test AI-generated code to ensure it fits your project's context and to learn from it, thereby improving your skills.

Question 3.7:
What is one way to improve the results you get when asking an AI for web code?
A) Ask one-word questions
B) Provide more context such as design style, target functionality, and examples
C) Limit yourself to one specific coding language
D) Use vague descriptions to see creative answers

Answer: B – Provide more context such as design style, target functionality, and examples
Explanation: Detailed and contextual prompts lead to higher-quality code suggestions from AI, making it easier to integrate them into your projects.

Chapter 4: How to Ask AI for HTML Code (7 Questions)

Question 4.1:
Which HTML element is used to create the main container for the content visible on a webpage?
A) <header>
B) <body>
C) <footer>
D) <section>

Answer: B – <body>
Explanation: The <body> element contains all the content that is visible on the page. It is the primary container for text, images, and other elements.

Question 4.2:
When asking AI to generate HTML code for a webpage, why is it important to be specific?
A) Specific prompts limit the creativity of the AI
B) Specific prompts help the AI provide more relevant and accurate code
C) Specific prompts slow down code generation
D) Specific prompts are only necessary for advanced users

Answer: B – Specific prompts help the AI provide more relevant and accurate code
Explanation: Detailed prompts give the AI the context it needs to generate code that meets your requirements, improving the quality of the output.

Question 4.3:
Which HTML tag is best suited for displaying a list of items with bullet points?
A) <ol>
B) <ul>
C) <div>
D) <span>

Answer: B – `<ul>`
Explanation: The `<ul>` (unordered list) tag is used to create lists with bullet points. Each item inside the list is typically wrapped in an `<li>` tag.

Question 4.4:
To add an image to your webpage using AI-generated HTML, which attribute is crucial for accessibility?
A) `class`
B) `src`
C) `alt`
D) `id`

Answer: C – `alt`
Explanation: The `alt` attribute provides alternative text for an image, which is important for accessibility and helps screen readers describe the image to users.

Question 4.5:
Which HTML tag is used to create hyperlinks?
A) `<hyperlink>`
B) `<link>`
C) `<a>`
D) `<nav>`

Answer: C – `<a>`
Explanation: The `<a>` tag is used to create hyperlinks. The destination URL is specified in the `href` attribute, which connects to another webpage or resource.

Question 4.6:
If you need AI to generate HTML code for a webpage with a header, paragraph, and image, which additional detail is most helpful to include in your prompt?
A) The color scheme of the website
B) The specific text for the header and paragraph
C) The font style of the text
D) The browser type you are using

Answer: B – The specific text for the header and paragraph
Explanation: Including detailed content requirements (like the exact text) helps the AI generate a more targeted and useful HTML code snippet.

Question 4.7:
What is the primary benefit of having an AI assistant generate HTML code for beginners?
A) It automatically creates complex server logic
B) It provides a step-by-step example that can be customized and learned from
C) It eliminates the need to learn coding entirely
D) It replaces the need for human creativity in design

Answer: B – It provides a step-by-step example that can be customized and learned from
Explanation: AI-generated code offers a practical starting point that beginners can review, customize, and learn from, thereby improving their understanding of HTML.

Chapter 5: How to Ask AI for CSS Styling (7 Questions)

Question 5.1:
What is the purpose of CSS in web design?
A) To add interactive functionality
B) To structure the content
C) To define the visual style and layout
D) To connect to databases

Answer: C – To define the visual style and layout
Explanation: CSS (Cascading Style Sheets) is used to style and arrange the visual aspects of a webpage, such as colors, fonts, spacing, and overall layout.

Question 5.2:
When asking AI for CSS code, which of the following details should you include?
A) The file size of your HTML document
B) Specific style preferences like colors, fonts, and layout styles
C) The operating system you are using
D) The name of your website only

Answer: B – Specific style preferences like colors, fonts, and layout styles
Explanation: Providing clear and detailed style requirements helps the AI generate CSS code that matches your design vision.

Question 5.3:
Which CSS property is used to change the color of text?
A) `background-color`
B) `font-size`
C) `color`
D) `margin`

Answer: C – `color`
Explanation: The `color` property in CSS sets the text color of an element.

Question 5.4:
What does the CSS property `background-color` control?
A) The color of the borders
B) The spacing around an element
C) The color behind an element's content
D) The font style

Answer: C – The color behind an element's content
Explanation: The `background-color` property sets the color of the background for an element.

Question 5.5:
Which CSS property would you use to make the layout of
your webpage responsive?
A) `transition`
B) `display: flex`
C) `color`
D) `font-family`

Answer: B – `display: flex`
Explanation: The Flexbox layout (using `display: flex`)
is a powerful tool for creating responsive and flexible
layouts that adjust smoothly across different screen sizes.

Question 5.6:
When customizing a button's hover effect in CSS, which
pseudo-class is used?
A) `:focus`
B) `:active`
C) `:hover`
D) `:visited`

Answer: C – `:hover`
Explanation: The `:hover` pseudo-class is used to define
the style that an element will have when the mouse pointer
hovers over it.

Question 5.7:
Why might you ask AI to generate a CSS snippet?
A) To avoid learning any CSS altogether
B) To receive a starting point that you can modify and learn
from
C) To ensure your website does not need any styling
D) To automatically handle server-side logic

Answer: B – To receive a starting point that you can modify and learn from

Explanation: AI-generated CSS provides an initial framework that you can build upon. It helps beginners see examples of good practices while allowing them to make customizations as needed.

Chapter 6: How to Ask AI for Simple JavaScript (7 Questions)

Question 6.1:
Which JavaScript method is most commonly used to attach an event handler to an element?
A) `getElementById`
B) `addEventListener`
C) `querySelector`
D) `innerHTML`

Answer: B – `addEventListener`

Explanation: The `addEventListener` method attaches an event handler to an element, allowing you to specify what should happen when the event (such as a click) occurs.

Question 6.2:
When asking AI for JavaScript to create interactivity, what is one useful detail to include in your prompt?
A) The color preferences for the website
B) The specific user interaction, such as "on click" or "on hover"
C) The file structure of your project
D) The number of HTML files used

Answer: B – The specific user interaction, such as "on click" or "on hover"

Explanation: Being specific about the interaction (for example, a button click triggering an alert) helps the AI generate precise JavaScript code suited to your needs.

Question 6.3:
Which of the following is an example of a simple JavaScript interaction?
A) Changing the background color of a webpage
B) Displaying an alert message when a button is clicked
C) Styling text using CSS
D) Creating a new HTML tag

Answer: B – Displaying an alert message when a button is clicked
Explanation: A common JavaScript interaction involves adding an event listener to a button that triggers an alert, demonstrating how users' actions can be responded to dynamically.

Question 6.4:
What is the purpose of using `preventDefault()` in a form submit event?
A) To automatically submit the form
B) To stop the form from being submitted until validation is complete
C) To style the form elements
D) To refresh the webpage

Answer: B – To stop the form from being submitted until validation is complete
Explanation: The `preventDefault()` method is used in event handling to cancel the default action (in this case, form submission) until your code determines that it is safe to proceed.

Question 6.5:
Why is it helpful for beginners to ask AI for JavaScript code examples?
A) It replaces the need for understanding how code works
B) It provides practical examples that can be studied and customized
C) It guarantees that the code will be error-free without modifications
D) It teaches advanced algorithms automatically

Answer: B – It provides practical examples that can be studied and customized
Explanation: AI-generated code examples serve as a learning tool; beginners can see how common functions are implemented and then modify them according to their own needs.

Question 6.6:
What is one common use of JavaScript in web pages as described in this chapter?
A) Structuring the HTML content
B) Adding interactivity like alerts and form validation
C) Styling the webpage elements
D) Hosting the website on a server

Answer: B – Adding interactivity like alerts and form validation
Explanation: JavaScript is used to add interactive elements — such as triggering alerts and validating forms — thus enhancing user experience.

Question 6.7:
Which of the following best describes a "prompt" when working with AI for code generation?
A) A command to compile your code
B) A detailed request that explains what code you need
C) An error message from the browser
D) A specific type of HTML tag

Answer: B – A detailed request that explains what code you need

Explanation: A prompt is the instruction you give the AI that details the functionality or design you want; the clearer you are, the better the AI's output will be.

Chapter 7: Building a Basic Web Page (7 Questions)

Question 7.1:

What is the purpose of the `<!DOCTYPE html>` declaration at the beginning of an HTML document?

A) To link the CSS file
B) To specify the HTML version being used
C) To create a navigation menu
D) To add JavaScript functionality

Answer: B – To specify the HTML version being used

Explanation: The `<!DOCTYPE html>` declaration tells the web browser to interpret the document as HTML5, ensuring proper rendering.

Question 7.2:

Which section of an HTML document contains metadata, including the title and links to external resources?

A) `<body>`
B) `<header>`
C) `<head>`
D) `<footer>`

Answer: C – `<head>`

Explanation: The `<head>` element houses metadata about the document, such as the title, character encoding, and links to CSS or JavaScript files.

Question 7.3:
How do you create a hyperlink in HTML that opens in a new browser tab?
A) `<a href="url" target="_blank">Link</a>`
B) `<link href="url" newtab="yes">Link</link>`
C) `<a newtab href="url">Link</a>`
D) `<a href="url">Link</a>`

Answer: A – `<a href="url" target="_blank">Link</a>`
Explanation: The `target="_blank"` attribute specifies that the linked document will open in a new browser tab or window.

Question 7.4:
Which HTML tag is used to insert an image into a webpage?
A) `<picture>`
B) `<image>`
C) `<img>`
D) `<src>`

Answer: C – `<img>`
Explanation: The `<img>` tag is used to embed images; it requires the `src` attribute for the image URL and the `alt` attribute for alternative text.

Question 7.5:
What is the purpose of adding comments inside HTML code?
A) To display extra text on the webpage
B) To provide notes or explanations in the code that are not rendered by the browser
C) To change the formatting of the HTML content
D) To link to external stylesheets

Answer: B – To provide notes or explanations in the code that are not rendered by the browser
Explanation: Comments (using `<!-- comment -->`) help developers understand the code and remind them of design decisions without affecting the webpage's display.

Question 7.6:
What is one benefit of testing your website in a browser as you develop it?
A) It increases the website's loading time
B) It immediately shows how changes in code affect the site's appearance and functionality
C) It disables interactive elements for debugging
D) It automatically fixes CSS errors

Answer: B – It immediately shows how changes in code affect the site's appearance and functionality
Explanation: Testing your website in a browser provides instant visual feedback, allowing you to quickly spot and correct mistakes.

Question 7.7:
When building a basic webpage, what element would you use to include a paragraph of text?
A) `<h1>`
B) `<div>`
C) `<p>`
D) `<span>`

Answer: C – `<p>`
Explanation: The `<p>` element is specifically designed to create paragraphs, grouping lines of text into a single block for clarity.

Chapter 8: Making It Beautiful with CSS (7 Questions)

Question 8.1:
Which two methods can you use to add CSS styles to your web page?
A) Inline styles and JavaScript
B) Style tags and external stylesheets
C) HTML tags and PHP scripts
D) JSON and XML files

Answer: B – Style tags and external stylesheets
Explanation: CSS can be applied directly within HTML using `<style>` tags in the head or via external stylesheets that are linked to the HTML file.

Question 8.2:
What is one advantage of using an external stylesheet over inline styles?
A) It makes the HTML file larger
B) It allows for styles to be reused across multiple pages
C) It prevents any CSS errors
D) It automatically generates responsive design

Answer: B – It allows for styles to be reused across multiple pages
Explanation: External stylesheets separate design from content, making it easier to maintain and apply consistent styles throughout your website.

Question 8.3:
Which CSS property would you use to change the font of text on your webpage?
A) `font-family`
B) `text-style`
C) `font-color`
D) `font-weight`

Answer: A – `font-family`

Explanation: The `font-family` property sets the typeface for text, helping define the overall style and readability of the content.

Question 8.4:

How does the `transition` property in CSS enhance user interaction?

A) By instantly changing styles without animation
B) By adding smooth animation effects when styles change
C) By encrypting user data
D) By automatically resizing images

Answer: B – By adding smooth animation effects when styles change

Explanation: The `transition` property enables a gradual change from one style property to another, creating smooth, visually appealing effects.

Question 8.5:

When adding an external stylesheet, which HTML tag is used?

A) `<script>`
B) `<style>`
C) `<link>`
D) `<css>`

Answer: C – `<link>`

Explanation: The `<link>` tag is used to include external resources such as CSS files in your HTML document.

Question 8.6:

In a responsive design, why are relative units like percentages or ems preferred over pixels?

A) They limit the design to desktop only
B) They allow the layout to adapt to different screen sizes
C) They create fixed-size elements
D) They are easier to type

Answer: B – They allow the layout to adapt to different screen sizes
Explanation: Relative units adjust based on the size of the device's screen, making the website more flexible and accessible on mobile and desktop devices.

Question 8.7:
What role can AI play when you ask for CSS design suggestions?
A) It prints your code on paper
B) It offers base styles and design templates that you can further customize
C) It removes the need to write HTML
D) It automatically publishes your website

Answer: B – It offers base styles and design templates that you can further customize
Explanation: AI can generate starter CSS designs based on your descriptions, providing you with a framework that you can tailor to suit your vision.

Chapter 9: Making It Interactive with JavaScript (7 Questions)

Question 9.1:
What HTML element is commonly used in JavaScript to capture user clicks?
A) `<p>`
B) `<button>`
C) `<img>`
D) `<div>`

Answer: B – `<button>`
Explanation: Buttons are frequently used in interactive web pages. By attaching JavaScript event listeners to `<button>` elements, you can trigger various actions like alerts or dynamic content updates.

Question 9.2:
Which method is used to display a popup message in JavaScript when a user clicks an element?
A) `console.log()`
B) `alert()`
C) `prompt()`
D) `confirm()`

Answer: B – `alert()`
Explanation: The `alert()` method displays a popup dialog box with a specified message, making it one of the simplest ways to provide feedback when an element is clicked.

Question 9.3:
In form validation using JavaScript, what is the common purpose of the `event.preventDefault()` method?
A) It changes the button color
B) It stops the default form submission until certain conditions are met
C) It automatically submits the form
D) It formats the input text

Answer: B – It stops the default form submission until certain conditions are met
Explanation: `event.preventDefault()` prevents the form's default action (submitting) so that you can perform validations or other actions before allowing the submission.

Question 9.4:
Which JavaScript property is used to change the text content of an HTML element?
A) `innerHTML`
B) `textContent`
C) `value`
D) `style`

Answer: B – `textContent`
Explanation: The `textContent` property is used to set or return the text content of an element, making it useful for dynamically updating content based on user interactions.

Question 9.5:
If you want a JavaScript function to execute when a button is clicked, which event is most appropriate?
A) `onload`
B) `onmouseover`
C) `onclick`
D) `onchange`

Answer: C – `onclick`
Explanation: The `onclick` event is used to trigger JavaScript code when the user clicks a button or clickable element.

Question 9.6:
How can AI help improve the interactive features on your website?
A) By automatically storing your data in a database
B) By generating code snippets that add dynamic interactions like alerts, toggles, and more
C) By removing the need for any JavaScript
D) By providing hosting services

Answer: B – By generating code snippets that add dynamic interactions like alerts, toggles, and more
Explanation: AI can generate simple JavaScript scripts that demonstrate common interactive features, which you can then modify and integrate into your website.

Question 9.7:

What is one benefit of using AI for JavaScript code generation?

A) It produces polished code that doesn't require any testing

B) It offers sample code that serves as a learning tool and starting point for customization

C) It replaces the need to understand JavaScript concepts

D) It only works with pre-defined website templates

Answer: B – It offers sample code that serves as a learning tool and starting point for customization

Explanation: AI-generated JavaScript code gives you a practical example to learn from and customize, helping to build both functionality and your understanding.

Chapter 10: Mini Website Projects with AI (7 Questions)

Question 10.1:

Which project type is best for showcasing your work and personal skills online?

A) A landing page

B) A portfolio page

C) A quiz game

D) A photo gallery

Answer: B – A portfolio page

Explanation: A personal portfolio page is designed to display your skills, projects, and experiences, making it ideal for showcasing your work to potential employers or clients.

Question 10.2:
What is a key feature you might include on a landing page for a product or event?
A) A complex database integration
B) A hero section with a compelling call-to-action
C) Advanced server-side logic
D) A multi-step checkout system

Answer: B – A hero section with a compelling call-to-action
Explanation: Landing pages commonly include a hero section that grabs visitors' attention and drives them toward a specific action, such as signing up or purchasing a product.

Question 10.3:
In an interactive quiz game website, which element is essential?
A) A static image gallery
B) A question and answer interface
C) A downloadable PDF document
D) A contact form

Answer: B – A question and answer interface
Explanation: A quiz game requires an interface that presents questions and possible answers, along with logic for validating responses and tracking scores.

Question 10.4:
Which project typically uses a lightbox effect to showcase images?
A) Personal blog
B) Photo gallery
C) Interactive quiz
D) Landing page

Answer: B – Photo gallery
Explanation: A photo gallery with a lightbox effect allows users to click on thumbnails and view enlarged images in an overlay for a better visual experience.

Question 10.5:
When integrating AI into a mini project, what is an important step?
A) Relying entirely on AI code without customization
B) Reviewing and customizing the AI-generated code to meet your specific needs
C) Disabling all manual coding
D) Ignoring error messages

Answer: B – Reviewing and customizing the AI-generated code to meet your specific needs
Explanation: AI tools provide a great starting point, but you should always review and tweak the code so that it perfectly aligns with your project requirements and style.

Question 10.6:
Which mini project is best suited for learning how to integrate interactive JavaScript functions?
A) Personal Portfolio Page
B) Simple Landing Page
C) Interactive Quiz Game Website
D) Photo Gallery

Answer: C – Interactive Quiz Game Website
Explanation: An interactive quiz game leverages JavaScript for event handling, dynamic content updates, and scoring systems — all of which are excellent for learning interactivity.

Question 10.7:
How does working on mini projects with AI benefit non-coders?
A) It eliminates all learning curves in web development
B) It provides practical experience by combining AI-generated code with personal customization
C) It forces you to memorize every line of code
D) It limits creative freedom

Answer: B – It provides practical experience by combining AI-generated code with personal customization

Explanation: Mini projects help non-coders apply theoretical knowledge and AI-generated code in real-world scenarios, making them more confident and skilled over time.

Chapter 11: How to Expand Projects (7 Questions)

Question 11.1:
What is a key benefit of turning your single-page website into a multi-page site?

A) It decreases site navigation

B) It organizes content into logical sections for better usability

C) It removes the need for CSS styling

D) It limits the amount of content you can display

Answer: B – It organizes content into logical sections for better usability

Explanation: Multi-page websites allow you to separate content into distinct sections, making it easier for users to find information and navigate the site.

Question 11.2:
Which HTML element is commonly used to create navigation menus across multiple pages?

A) <nav>

B) <section>

C) <footer>

D) <aside>

Answer: A – <nav>

Explanation: The <nav> element is specifically designed for grouping navigation links, making it an ideal choice for multi-page websites.

Question 11.3:

What is the main purpose of CSS media queries in responsive design?
A) To add backend functionality
B) To alter styles based on the screen size or device characteristics
C) To change HTML content dynamically
D) To manage database connections

Answer: B – To alter styles based on the screen size or device characteristics
Explanation: Media queries in CSS enable you to modify the layout and styling of your website based on the device's width, ensuring a responsive design.

Question 11.4:

Which of the following is an example of a free hosting service for front-end projects?
A) GitHub Pages
B) Amazon Web Services
C) Microsoft SQL Server
D) Oracle DB

Answer: A – GitHub Pages
Explanation: GitHub Pages offers free hosting for static websites, making it an excellent choice for beginners looking to publish their projects online.

Question 11.5:

When asking AI for "next steps" to upgrade a site, what key detail should you include?
A) The current functionality and design of your site
B) Only the target audience demographic
C) A complete replacement of your HTML structure
D) The total number of pages on your website

Answer: A – The current functionality and design of your site
Explanation: Providing details about your site's current state helps the AI suggest realistic and relevant improvements.

Question 11.6:
What does making a website "responsive" mean?
A) It responds only to keyboard inputs
B) It automatically adjusts its layout for different screen sizes
C) It uses fixed pixel sizes for all elements
D) It eliminates the use of images

Answer: B – It automatically adjusts its layout for different screen sizes
Explanation: A responsive website dynamically adapts its layout and design to provide an optimal viewing experience on desktops, tablets, and phones.

Question 11.7:
Which technique can help you upgrade your site as you gain more experience?
A) Ignoring feedback
B) Relying only on outdated code
C) Asking AI for suggestions on additional features and improvements
D) Avoiding any changes to the original design

Answer: C – Asking AI for suggestions on additional features and improvements
Explanation: Using AI to inquire about "next steps" encourages continuous improvement and helps you learn about new features or techniques to enhance your website.

Chapter 12: Understanding and Editing AI Code (7 Questions)

Question 12.1:
What is one of the main goals when reviewing AI-generated code?
 A) Memorizing the code exactly as it is
 B) Understanding how the code works so you can modify it
 C) Replacing it entirely with handwritten code
 D) Ignoring comments and context

Answer: B – Understanding how the code works so you can modify it
Explanation: The primary goal is to learn from the AI-generated code by analyzing its structure and logic, which empowers you to make custom changes.

Question 12.2:
Which of the following is a benefit of editing AI-generated code rather than using it verbatim?
 A) It makes the code less efficient
 B) It helps you tailor the code to your specific project needs and enhances your learning
 C) It prevents you from understanding the fundamentals
 D) It leads to untestable code

Answer: B – It helps you tailor the code to your specific project needs and enhances your learning
Explanation: Editing code forces you to engage with it deeply, helping you understand key concepts and allowing you to create personalized solutions.

Question 12.3:
When viewing HTML, CSS, and JavaScript together, what should you look for first?
 A) The file names
 B) How the structure (HTML), styling (CSS), and behavior (JavaScript) interact
 C) The number of comments
 D) The browser version

Answer: B – How the structure (HTML), styling (CSS), and behavior (JavaScript) interact

Explanation: Understanding the relationship between these three components is key to diagnosing issues and making effective customizations.

Question 12.4:

Why is it beneficial to experiment with small changes in AI-generated code?

A) It discourages further learning

B) It allows you to see how different modifications impact functionality and design

C) It always results in errors

D) It makes the code unreadable

Answer: B – It allows you to see how different modifications impact functionality and design

Explanation: Experimenting with small changes helps you understand the code's behavior and improve your troubleshooting skills.

Question 12.5:

Which approach is recommended when you encounter a piece of code you don't understand?

A) Delete the code immediately

B) Analyze and research each part to learn its purpose

C) Copy and paste it without further investigation

D) Rely only on AI suggestions without questioning

Answer: B – Analyze and research each part to learn its purpose

Explanation: Breaking down and understanding each part of the code helps you learn coding principles and prevents future issues.

Question 12.6:
How does adding your own custom touches to AI-generated code benefit your projects?
A) It makes your projects less secure
B) It personalizes the project and enhances your understanding of coding concepts
C) It causes the code to run slower
D) It makes it harder for others to read your code

Answer: B – It personalizes the project and enhances your understanding of coding concepts
Explanation: Customization not only makes your website unique but also deepens your learning by forcing you to engage with and modify the code.

Question 12.7:
What does "learning from examples, not memorizing" mean in the context of coding?
A) Copying code without understanding
B) Studying how code works and adapting it, rather than trying to remember every detail
C) Ignoring best practices
D) Memorizing every single line of code

Answer: B – Studying how code works and adapting it, rather than trying to remember every detail
Explanation: Understanding the logic and structure behind code examples allows you to apply concepts to new situations, making you a more versatile developer.

Chapter 13: Solving Problems When Things Break (7 Questions)

Question 13.1:
When you encounter an error in your code, what is the first step you should take?
A) Immediately rewrite the entire code
B) Read the error message carefully to identify the issue
C) Ignore the error and hope it fixes itself
D) Delete all your work

Answer: B – Read the error message carefully to identify the issue
Explanation: Error messages often provide critical information that helps pinpoint the exact problem; starting here saves time and directs your troubleshooting efforts.

Question 13.2:
Which tool is most helpful for reviewing errors in your code during runtime?
A) A text editor's spell check
B) The browser's developer console
C) A word processor
D) Social media

Answer: B – The browser's developer console
Explanation: The developer console (accessed with F12 or "Inspect") displays error messages and logs that help diagnose issues in HTML, CSS, and JavaScript.

Question 13.3:
What does the function `preventDefault()` do in an event handler?
A) Stops the default action (e.g., form submission) from occurring
B) Automatically corrects errors
C) Refreshes the webpage
D) Converts text to uppercase

Answer: A – Stops the default action (e.g., form submission) from occurring
Explanation: `preventDefault()` cancels the default behavior of an event, allowing you to perform custom validations or actions first.

Question 13.4:
Which of the following is a common mistake made by beginners in HTML?
A) Using `<p>` for paragraphs
B) Forgetting to close tags
C) Using CSS for styling
D) Adding a `<title>` in the head section

Answer: B – Forgetting to close tags
Explanation: Unclosed tags can disrupt the structure of your page and cause rendering issues, making it one of the most frequent errors for beginners.

Question 13.5:
How can AI assist when you are stuck with a debugging problem?
A) It provides a detailed explanation and potential fix for your error
B) It automatically posts your error online
C) It deletes your code
D) It replaces your project entirely

Answer: A – It provides a detailed explanation and potential fix for your error
Explanation: A well-crafted debugging prompt to an AI can yield suggestions and corrections, guiding you to a solution while teaching you about the error.

Question 13.6:
Why should you view every error as a learning opportunity?
A) Errors can be ignored without consequence
B) Each error helps you understand more about how your code works and improve your skills
C) Errors reduce the performance of your website
D) Errors are a sign that you should stop coding

Answer: B – Each error helps you understand more about how your code works and improve your skills
Explanation: Embracing errors as learning experiences leads to a deeper understanding of programming concepts and better problem-solving abilities.

Question 13.7:
What is a useful strategy if you cannot identify the source of an error?
A) Comment out sections of code to isolate the problematic part
B) Reboot your computer immediately
C) Delete all of your code and start over
D) Ignore the error until it disappears

Answer: A – Comment out sections of code to isolate the problematic part
Explanation: Isolating parts of your code by commenting them out helps narrow down where the error is occurring, making it easier to diagnose and fix.

Chapter 14: Your Next Steps (7 Questions)

Question 14.1:
What is website hosting?
A) The process of designing a website
B) The process of storing website files on a server so that they are accessible online
C) The act of writing HTML code
D) A method for styling web pages

Answer: B – The process of storing website files on a server so that they are accessible online
Explanation: Hosting involves placing your website's files on a server that is connected to the internet, so that users can visit your site via a URL.

Question 14.2:
Which of the following is a free hosting option for static websites?
A) GitHub Pages
B) Microsoft Azure
C) Amazon EC2
D) Google Cloud Platform

Answer: A – GitHub Pages
Explanation: GitHub Pages is a free hosting service ideal for static websites (HTML, CSS, and JavaScript), making it accessible for beginners.

Question 14.3:
What are CSS media queries used for?
A) To structure content on a webpage
B) To change styles based on screen size and device characteristics
C) To add dynamic functionality
D) To store images

Answer: B – To change styles based on screen size and device characteristics
Explanation: Media queries allow the application of different CSS rules depending on the device's width or other features, ensuring that your website is responsive.

Question 14.4:
Which advanced topic involves retrieving external data to display on your website?
A) Animations
B) APIs
C) Flexbox
D) Grid layouts

Answer: B – APIs
Explanation: APIs (Application Programming Interfaces) allow your website to request and display data from external sources, such as weather information or news updates.

Question 14.5:
What is Bootstrap primarily used for?
A) Hosting websites
B) Creating responsive and modern designs quickly using pre-built components
C) Writing server-side code
D) Generating dynamic JavaScript animations

Answer: B – Creating responsive and modern designs quickly using pre-built components
Explanation: Bootstrap is a CSS framework that provides ready-made components and grid systems to help designers quickly build attractive, responsive websites.

Question 14.6:
How can AI inspire creativity in your website projects?
A) By providing generic templates only
B) By generating custom design ideas and suggestions based on your prompts
C) By replacing your need to write any custom code
D) By limiting design options to pre-approved styles

Answer: B – By generating custom design ideas and suggestions based on your prompts
Explanation: AI can offer creative inspiration through code samples and design suggestions that you can adapt and personalize, encouraging innovative solutions.

Question 14.7:
What does "continuous improvement" mean in the context of web development?
A) Once the website is built, it should never be modified
B) Regularly updating and refining your website to improve functionality, design, and user experience
C) Only changing the color scheme occasionally
D) Deleting old projects and starting fresh every time

Answer: B – Regularly updating and refining your website to improve functionality, design, and user experience
Explanation: Continuous improvement involves making incremental updates to your website based on feedback, testing, and new learning—enhancing the overall quality and performance over time.

Bonus Section: Cheat Sheets for Non-Coders (2 Questions)

Question Bonus 1:
Which of the following lists contains the top HTML tags that you'll use most frequently according to the cheat sheet?
A) `<html>`, `<head>`, `<body>`, `<table>`, `<form>`
B) `<html>`, `<head>`, `<body>`, `<h1>-<h6>`, `<p>`, `<a>`, `<img>`, `<ul>`, `<ol>`, `<li>`, `<div>`, `<span>`
C) `<div>`, `<span>`, `<script>`, `<style>`, `<link>`
D) `<header>`, `<footer>`, `<section>`, `<article>`, `<nav>`

Answer: B
Explanation: The cheat sheet for non-coders recommends the top 10 HTML tags that include `<html>`, `<head>`, `<body>`, heading tags (`<h1>-<h6>`), `<p>`, `<a>`, `<img>`, list tags (`<ul>`, `<ol>`, `<li>`), `<div>`, and `<span>`. These tags form the basic building blocks used in most web projects.

Question Bonus 2:
What is one example of a JavaScript trick for beginners provided in the cheat sheet?
A) Using `fetch()` for server-side encryption
B) Toggling a class on an element to change its appearance dynamically
C) Creating SQL queries to retrieve data
D) Designing HTML layouts using JavaScript

Answer: B – Toggling a class on an element to change its appearance dynamically
Explanation: Among the JavaScript tricks for beginners, one example given is using `classList.toggle()` to add or remove a class from an element on certain user actions, which is a simple and effective way to create dynamic effects.

Final Thoughts

These 100 questions span across every chapter — from the basics of front-end development to troubleshooting and creative expansion. Each question is designed not only to test your knowledge but also to provide detailed explanations that help you understand the underlying concepts. By working through these questions, you should feel more confident in using AI to write, modify, and enhance your website code.

Happy coding, and may these cheat sheets and questions serve as a valuable resource throughout your web development journey!

Conclusion: About the Author – Laurence Svekis

Laurence Svekis is a passionate web development educator, industry innovator, and advocate for making technology accessible to everyone. With over two decades of experience in digital design, front-end development, and emerging technologies, Laurence has dedicated his career to breaking down complex coding concepts into digestible, beginner-friendly lessons. His journey from traditional coding to embracing AI-assisted development has inspired countless non-coders to take the leap into the world of website creation.

Born with a deep curiosity for how things work, Laurence began his career as a self-taught programmer before refining his skills at prestigious institutions and working alongside top technology companies.

Throughout his career, Laurence has developed a reputation for his clear communication, patient teaching style, and ability to demystify advanced topics through practical, real-world examples. His work leverages AI to simplify the process of coding, empowering beginners by providing them with a supportive learning environment and step-by-step guidance. Laurence's innovative approach has not only transformed the learning experience for aspiring developers but has also paved the way for more collaborative and accessible tech education.

Outside the realm of programming, Laurence is an active contributor to online tech communities, a mentor for young developers, and a frequent speaker at industry conferences where he shares his insights on AI in web development. His commitment to continuous learning and creativity fuels his ongoing projects, ensuring that his educational materials evolve with the rapidly changing landscape of digital technology.

Laurence Svekis aims to instill confidence, creativity, and practical skills in every reader. His comprehensive guide not only covers the technical aspects of HTML, CSS, and JavaScript but also empowers you to harness AI effectively, troubleshoot common issues, and expand your projects into fully functional websites. His belief that "every expert was once a beginner" resonates through every chapter, inspiring you to explore, experiment, and grow as a web developer.

As you continue your journey through web development, let Laurence's experience and passion for technology serve as your guiding light. Whether you're here to build your own portfolio, create a landing page for a project, or simply explore the fascinating world of coding, remember that with perseverance, creativity, and the right guidance, you can transform your ideas into dynamic, engaging websites.